Understanding
Chinese Characters
by their ancestral forms

Revised Second Edition

by
Ping-gam Go

Simplex Publications, San Francisco

To my daughters
Sian, Lan, and Hian

Understanding Chinese Characters by means of their ancestral forms. Copyright © 1988 Gam P. Go. Second Edition 1992.

This edition is an expansion and revision of a work previously published as **How to Understand Chinese Characters by means of their ancestral forms,** copyright © 1987, published by Simplex Publications, 11 Hugo Street, San Francisco, CA 94122, U.S.A.

ISBN: 0-9623113-1-6
First printing, 1988
Second printing, 1989

Printed in the U.S.A.

Contents

Acknowledgments

I would like to acknowledge my three daughters Sian, Lan and Hian for their keen interest in the project and for their valuable contributions in submitting material for the manuscript and in making suggestions, corrections and improvements. In addition to this, Lan took part in the editing of the second edition; she also spent many hours of tediously cutting and accurately replacing the Chinese characters in the Subject Index and in the Table of Contents.

Janet Gardiner did the difficult proofreading of the Chinatown Walk chapter. Emily Wilcox was very helpful in putting critical portions of the text in correct and clear language.

George Yasukochi wrote a detailed analysis of the book with valuable suggestions for changes.

The brush-written characters (not the ancestral forms, which were done by myself) was the work of You-shan Tang, calligrapher.

Bill Regan, Sr., Bill Regan, Jr., and Bert Ripple, through their interests and enthusiasms for the book in its early years, were instrumental in its gradual development.

Last but not least, Jean and Sara Gabriel of European Book Company, Inc. gave valuable suggestions as to the format and marketing of the book when it first came out as "How to Understand Chinese Characters" in 1987.

To all of them, I would like to express my sincere gratitude and thanks.

Notes on the Second Edition

To make it easy to find sections in the *Walk through Chinatown* text frequently referred to in the book, the **key characters are placed in boxes alongside the paragraphs in which they occur.** Also, you will find **new characters** discussed in the first part of the Photo Section.

All characters in the Character Finder are accompanied by their meanings. In many cases, you only want to know their meanings, and this arrangement makes it in such cases unnecessary for you to consult the Dictionary. (Through the character numbers you can still find their additional meanings and their etymology in the Dictionary.)

To locate a character in the Character Finder, you have to know the number of strokes it contains. In **"How to Use the Character Finder"**, **you will find complete information on writing a Chinese character and on finding the number of strokes it contains.**

An important addition has been made inasmuch as **references to the photographs have been introduced in the Dictionary Section.** The quality of the photographs has been highly improved by printing them through metal plates; and **new photos** have been introduced.

Following consultation with *A Chinese-English Dictionary,* published by the Beijing Foreign Language Institute, **additional meanings** have been introduced in the Dictionary Section and in the Subject Index.

And finally, in the Table of Contents and in the Subject Index **all Chinese characters have been replaced by bigger and better ones.**

Foreword

A number of books have been written dealing with the origin of Chinese characters. They explain the meaning of the modern brush writings on the basis of their ancestral forms. All are ultimately based on the classical lexicon *Shuo Wên Chieh Tzu* (freely translated: "On the interpretation of characters") written around the year 200 A.D. by a famous scholar named Hsü-hsên. It is the oldest Chinese dictionary on record, now simply known as the *Shuo Wên*. To this day it has formed the basis of all research in etymology.

You will discover that it takes little effort and imagination to understand the most commonly seen characters, once you know their ancestral forms and their explanations.

This book is a follow-up course to my other book, *Read Chinese Today*, which discusses 68 common characters. In this book you will find the ancestral forms and explanations of 288 characters. With a knowledge of these characters, you will be able to understand most of the beautiful Chinese characters in San Francisco's Chinatown and in other American cities.

Introduction

Chinese characters – let's understand them !

Contrary to general belief, the Chinese writing system is not a complex system to be understood only by the Chinese . Far from that – it is an amazingly simple system which reveals the ingenuity of the ancient Chinese scholars. The complexity came about only after the writing brush transformed the original stylus pictures into puzzling entities.

The origin of Chinese characters goes far back to the early history of China some 5,000 years ago, around 3000 B.C., as can be established from inscriptions on oracle bones made of tortoise shells. During a later period, inscriptions were made on sacrificial vessels as a means to establish contact with the spirits of deceased loved ones. It was probably due to the need to communicate with invisible deities and spirits that a stylus writing system consisting of pictures and symbols was created.

The first emperor of China, Huang-ti (ca. 2600 B.C.) ordered one of his talented officials to develop a more simplified writing system. The resulting series of drawings can be regarded as the earliest Chinese characters. These drawings triggered many changes toward simpler forms for easier writing, resulting in a multiform writing system, since each state adopted its own. During the reign of emperor Ch'in Shih-huang (246–214 B.C.), who linked together all sectional walls into what is now known as the Great Wall, one Prime Minister Li-ssu advised the emperor to forbid the use of characters which differed from the ones officially used in the empire. A uniform writing system of drawings was therefore established.

During the same period, however, a prison inspector obtained permission from the emperor to introduce a new and entirely different method using a writing brush, earlier invented by a general named Mêng-t'ien. It was soon widely accepted as the ideal system, because writing with the brush using ink and paper was much faster than writing with the stylus on bamboo or wood. However, the ease with which characters could be written has its drawbacks. It led to alterations of the originals, deviating more and more from the original stylus writings. *Also, because the brush could not make adequate drawings, new drawings were rarely created. New characters were formed consisting of two existing drawings: one gives the general idea of the meaning, the other gives the pronunciation of the character.*

Toward the year 200 A.D., a scholar named Hsü-shên, after long journeys to obtain original stylus writings, wrote a lexicon with short explanatory notes of most characters known at that time. His purpose was to prevent the progressive alteration of the characters, by displaying their authentic forms to all scholars. Called the *Shuo Wên Chieh Tzu* ("On the interpretation of characters") or simply the *Shuo Wên* , it has since been the bible among etymologists.

Why characters are difficult to understand, unless we know their ancestral forms.

The brush writings are only approximations of the stylus drawings, because unlike the stylus, the writing brush cannot make the loops and intricate details that the drawings contain. Also, over the course of time, new types of brush-written characters were introduced by famous scholars. As a result the system has gradually lost its value of being one based on easily understandable drawings, which the old stylus-written system was. On the following pages, examples of the old script are shown which contain excellent information about their meanings, whereas the new script offers little or none whatsoever.

Probably the best examples are given by No.2 and No.3 seen together. The stylus gives an excellent picture of a **Woman** 足 (No.2); by adding two small strokes, the breasts are formed and a picture of **Mother** 足 (No.3) is obtained. The brush-written forms are 女 and 母 : two completely unrelated forms which offer little clue about their meanings.

The stylus gives exquisite portrayals of the **Horse** 馬 (No.4) and the **Bird** 鳥 (No. 5). The brush writings are clumsy, meaningless imitations: 馬 and 鳥 . Nor can the brush draw the pictures for **Music. Joy** 樂 (a musical instrument, No.8) and **Ten thousand** 萬 (a scorpion, No.9), because it cannot draw the small bells and the claws.

Similar remarks can be made with regard to the remaining examples. The stylus drawings reveal the ingenuity and resourcefulness of the ancient Chinese scholars, as can be best be seen in: **Friend** 友 (No.12), **Morning** 朝 (No.13), **West** 西 (No.15), **Gold** 金 (No.16), **Island** 島 (No.17), **Traveler** 旅 (No.19) and **All.The people** 衆 (No.20).

The following characters are among the most common and can be seen quite often: 龍 **Dragon** (No.10), **Gold** 金 (No.16), **China** 華 (No.21), **Double joy** 囍 (No.24), **Prosperous** 興 (No.26), **Longevity** 壽 (No.30). None of them contain information about its meaning , which can easily be obtained from its ancestral form.

1		Picture of the heart with the sac opened; the lobes and the aorta are also seen. **Heart**	心
2		Picture of a woman with a curvy figure. **Woman**	女
3		Picture of a woman 丸 with breasts added. **Mother**	母
4		Picture of a horse with its mane blowing in the wind. **Horse**	馬
5		Picture of a bird. **Bird**	鳥
6		Picture of a fish: head 𠂊 , scaly body ⊘ , and tail ⌇ . **Fish**	魚
7		Picture of a flying crane. **To fly**	飛
8		A musical instrument: a frame with a drum (in the middle) and bells (on the sides). **Music. Joy**	樂
9		Picture of a scorpion with its head ⊗ , legs and tail ⱦ⫰ and its "thousands" of claws ⱱ. **Ten thousand**	萬
10		A dragon 丸 flying toward the sky = and its wings 彡 . (It was believed that dragons flew to the sky and produced rain). **Dragon**	龍

11		An upward-flying bird with wings backward, trying in vain to reach the sky −. **Not. No**	不
12		Two hands working in the same direction. **Friend**	友
13		When the sun ⊖ has risen to the height of a man's helmet. **Morning**	早
14		Locks of hair so long that it must be tied with a band − and a brooch. **Long**	長
15		When birds sit on their nests, it is evening and the sun is in the West. **West**	西
16		Four nuggets buried (∧ to cover) in the earth ±. **Gold. Metal**	金
17		A mountain in the sea, on which birds can rest while crossing it. **Island**	島
18		The sun θ and the sprouting of plants (plants). **Spring**	春
19		Transients (men) seeking shelter under the overhanging branches ∧ of a wind-blown tree. **Traveler**	旅
20		A crowd (men) as observed by the eye. **All. The people**	眾

21		Leaves and flowers that are expanding into full bloom. **China**	華
22		Soot deposited around the aperture by a smoky fire. **Black**	黑
23		There is singing (mouth) and music (hand with a stick – beating a drum on a stand). **Joy**	喜
24		Joy (see No. 23) repeated twice. **Double joy**	囍
25		The child in darkness (a small room) and two hands of the master pouring knowledge . **Learn. Science**	學
26		Two pair of hands lifting up an object harmoniously (cover fits vessel's mouth). **Prosperous. Flourishing**	興
27		A multitude (= ++++ = forty) of men clearing a forest (many trees). **Not. Without**	無
28		A pot with contents , a ladle , and the symbol to suggest mixing (three lines coming together). **Food**	食
29		Food (see No. 28) and a hand in motion , bringing the food into one's mouth. **Cooked rice. Meal**	飯
30		White hair (hair , change), wrinkles (furrows), to implore (mouth, hand) for long life. **Longevity**	壽

A Walk through San Francisco's Chinatown

The following pages explain the meanings of commonly seen Chinese characters on the basis of their ancestral forms. San Francisco's Chinatown offers a unique opportunity to study them. Knowing their meanings will allow you to really appreciate their beauty. It is not necessary for you to do the actual walk. This chapter and the accompanying photos in the **Photo Section** (**"Getting to know them"**, on page P1) containing multi-choice questions, gives you the means to become familiar with them.

Read Chinese Today, my other book, takes you to an armchair or actual walk through San Francisco's Chinatown and offers you an opportunity to be quite familiar with 68 of the most commonly seen characters, through questions and answers given to you during the walk.

I. A Walk through San Francisco's Chinatown.

A short walk through San Francisco's Chinatown will allow us to study and understand 68 common characters. They are very common characters that are used over and over again by the Chinese.

The Entrance Gate to Chinatown bears a sign with a well-known saying by Confucius*: 公 為 下 天 , which written in their ancestral forms would be: 小 鬲 丁 禾 . Old Chinese writings are read from right to left**. So the first character is 禾 , which means <u>HEAVEN</u> [i.e. *that which expands* ⁻ *over* **Man** 大 (*a Man with widespread arms and legs*)].
The second character is 丁 , which means <u>BELOW</u> (*an object | below a certain level* ⁻). The third character was originally written 鬲 . It is a picture of a **Female Monkey** with its *claws* 爪 , *body* 宀 and *breasts* 八 . The original meaning of this character is lost, but one of its present meanings is <u>FOR</u> (**For the benefit of**). Lastly, the last character 小 means <u>COMMON</u>, or <u>PUBLIC</u>. It represents the *division/distribution* 八 *of private property* (厶 *cocoon,* with the self-enclosed silkworm it gives the idea of privacy *) among the common people.*
Putting the four meanings together, we would have " Below Heaven For Common". Freely translated it would be: "<u>Under Heaven We All Must Work for the Common Good</u>"(Photo A)

---

* This saying was quoted by **Dr. Sun Yat-Sen** [who led the Revolution that overthrew the Manchu Dynasty (1644–1912)] in one of a series of lectures that he held one year before his death in 1925.

** Writing was done on a roll of paper or silk, with the right hand doing the writing and the left hand holding the roll and unrolling the material. Therefore, writing was done from right to left.

Let us now see characters that we see a lot of times. For instance, we will quite often see these two characters next to each other: 酒家. Originally they were written: 酒家. The first means **Wine** : a *wine jar* and *wine* (*liquid*); the other one means **House(hold)**: a *dwelling* where *pigs* 豕 had free entry ***. The two characters combined mean <u>**Wine House**</u> or <u>RESTAURANT</u> , namely *one that serves liquor.* (**Photos B,E,G,K**).

The Chinese have other notations for Restaurants. They often use 宮 if it is big and stylish.It means <u>Palace</u> because the original writing is a *dwelling* containing a series of (a lot of) rooms . Smaller places quite often call themselves <u>Garden</u> 園 , which was originally written : an *enclosure* , and the symbol inside it, which means *a long robe** , because the long vines in the garden give the impression as if the trees put on long robes. (**Photo K: Palace**),(**Photos B,O,M: Garden**).

A bigger restaurant with *dining rooms upstairs,* will use 樓 : a <u>Multi-Story Building</u> . The ancestral form of this character : a building (*tree* ,*wood*) and (a *woman* *locked* up in a *lofty palace prison* for misbehavior)(**Photo F**).

Another notation is 飯店; originally written the pair means <u>Rice Shop</u> , because the first is the symbol for **Food** or **Cooked Rice** : a *pot with contents* , a *ladle* and the symbol - three lines coming together -

---

* The symbol represents the *shoulder* on which the robe rests; the robe is so long that it is *dragging* (a *hook* attached to the harness, used for dragging objects) over the floor.

** This symbol represents *cracks* in a tortoise-shell which resulted when it was heated. Divination (fortune-telling) was then spoken out (*mouth*) after closely studying the cracks.

*** To make sure that they were adequately fed.

to suggest *mixing* ; and ⺀ is a *hand* in *motion* ∫ which brings the food into one's mouth. The second character ⟨占⟩ stands for **Shop** (∩ *shelter* in which *divination* ** 占 is practiced). **(Photo S, in Flower** *Shop*.**)**

店

Another combination we'll see is 餐 廳 , of which the ancestral forms are 飠 廰. The first character consists of many symbols, namely 飠 *food* (a *pot with contents* ⊖ , a *ladle* ⼔ , and ⌃ : three lines coming together to suggest *mixing*) ; 歺 a *skeleton* after the flesh is removed (by a *hand* ⺕). All of them put together they mean **Meal.** How about the other one ? A very complex one , it means **Hall.** It is composed of the symbol ∫ *shelter* and a very complicated portion 聽 , which means *to hear* and only serves as a "phonetic" (to give the pronunciation of the character). It is used here, because musical performance often takes place here. The two characters combined mean Meal Hall , or **Restaurant.** They are often used, because they look very beautiful and distinguished and give a certain dignity to the place. **(Photo T).**

餐

廳

Now that we have learned to understand these characters for "Restaurant", can we remember all of them ? The answer should be "Certainly!", especially if we live in San Francisco, because as can be expected, all these characters appear *at the end of the signs* and we can see and recognize them each time we visit Chinatown !

Here are other "pairs" that we can spot easily. Anywhere we go, we will find these two together: 公 司 , because they mean **FIRM** or **COMPANY**. In their ancestral forms they would look like this: 公 司 . The first means **Common**: a *division and distribution* 八 of private property 厶 (picture of a *cocoon* ; with the self-enclosed silkworm, it gives the idea of 'privacy'). The second symbol 司 is a *man bending over* ⺄ (⼈*man) *in order to shout his orders* (⼝ mouth), and means **To manage**

公

司

---
* See Footnote on page W6. ** See Footnote on page W4.

or **Administration**. Combining the two together, we have **Common Administration**. And is this not the idea behind a Firm or Company ? **(Photo I)**

Another pair that we'll see is that which indicates a **BANK.** This pair 銀行 we'll see often enough. It means **Silver Store**, because probably silver was the metal used as currency. (Gold being only used for decorative purposes and in jewelry.) **Silver** was originally written 鎁. It consists of two parts. The first part is 金 *metal***: 金 *four pieces of ore buried* (∧ *cover*) *in the ground*. The other part is 艮 : *a man* 人* *turning around* ⌐ , *in order to look another man 'defiantly' in the eye* 目 . The two parts combined mean **Silver**, because silver is malleable and 'defies' the action of a hammer. **Store** was originally written 行 , to mean *footsteps* ⼻ *made by left* (*and right* \ *feet*, and represents "a place where people come and go".
(Photo C: Bank) (Photo U: Herb Store)

銀

行

Walking through Chinatown, we will occasionally see these three characters next to each other displayed in the window of a restaurant 粥 麵 飯 **(PhotoV)**. Written in their ancestral forms they would look like this: . The first one means **PORRIDGE**: *Rice* 米 (*four grains of rice that are scattered* 小 *due to thrashing* 十) *that are thoroughly boiled* (*steam* 弓弓 *coming from boiling water*). The second character means **NOODLES**. It consists of two portions, of which the second (面 *face*) only serves as a "phonetic", to give the pronunciation of the character. The first portion 麥 means *Wheat* : *a plant* 火 (picture of a plant with its *trunk* | *branches* ∨ and *roots* ∩) *with ears of grain* 人人; *and* 夊 which is a *man* 人 * *who advances* 刀 * *in spite of obstacles* ∧

粥

麵

---

* *The being that has two legs* 人 - only the legs are portrayed. *A man who 'advances'*: a man 人 deformed 刀 , because of his movement. (see last sentence of this page).
** If standing by itself, this symbol means **Gold**.

suggesting the relentless development of the grain. The third character, as we already discussed under "Restaurant", means **COOKED RICE**.**Having displayed "Porridge, Noodles and Rice (plates)", the place wants to tell the public that it serves all the dishes the public desires, including porridge, which is rarely served in other restaurants. 飯

Another pair of characters that we'll see is that which shows that a restaurant serves **DIM SUM** 點 心 the Cantonese pastry lunch that is very popular in San Francisco, also among tourists **(Photo D).** The original writing would be: 點 心 . The second character is a picture of the **Heart** : it shows the *sac* (opened), the *lobes* and *aorta*. The first character means **Speck** or **Dot**. It consists of two parts: the first part 黑 means black (*soot* ✕ deposited by a *smoky fire* 炎 around a *vent* ⊕); the second part serves only as a "phonetic", giving an indication how to pronounce the character. The two characters combined mean literally " speck heart ", which freely translated would be "a little heartiness" or simply "a snack" as we say it. 心 點

Several times during the walk, we will encounter the character 華 , which stands for **CHINA (Photos B,P,Q).**
Originally written 華 , it actually means **Glorious**, being a picture of *a branch with leaves and flowers* ✿ *expanding* 亐 * *into full bloom.* It became a symbol for **China.** Usually, however, it is accompanied by another character 中 **Center** (originally 中 : *a target* 口 *that is pierced in the center by an arrow* 丨), because for the Chinese, China was the center of the World. **(Photos P,Q).** 華 中

Often, therefore, we also find the combination 中 國 , which means **Center Country**, to stand for **China**. Originally **Country** was written 或 : *a bordered piece of land* 國

---

* Breath 𝄖 after passing an obstacle ⎯, *expanding* freely.
** See pp. **W**4, **W**5, **W**12

☐ *defended by weapons (⽧ halberd) with a capital ○.* **(Photos C,U)**

Now that we know how the Chinese write "China", we would like to know how they write **AMERICA** ! We see it on the sign for the Bank of America: 美國銀行 . **(Photo C)** The last two characters mean **Bank**, we know from the above.** The second character we just met: **Country.** The first 美 means **Beautiful**. Originally written 美 , it is composed of *sheep* ⽺ (picture of a sheep, seen from behind, showing the *horns* Υ , *four feet and tail* ⼿) and *big* 大 (a man with outstretched arms, as if he wants to show how big something is), to give the meaning **Beautiful**(*a big sheep being a beautiful animal*). Combining the two characters together we get **Beautiful Country.**

During our walk, we will see a number of very common characters. These are *good luck signs* that we see in the shop windows, especially those of jewelry stores. One that we very often see is 壽 **LONGEVITY** . The ancestral form is 𧶠 which consists of five symbols compressed into one. Two symbols are combined to form **Old**: *hair* ⼭ and *change* ⼈ (a man* ⼈ who is upside down ⼉ , who *changed* his position), giving the idea of '*white hair*'. The third symbol Ɀ represents **wrinkles** found on an old person's face. The remaining two symbols ⼝ *mouth* and ⼹ *hand* are to give the idea of "making a wish using gestures", or "to wish deeply". To conclude therefore, we may say that the character means "**longevity following a deep wish**". **(Photo W4)**

Another character that we'll meet quite often is 囍. It means **DOUBLE JOY** and is usually used to celebrate a wedding. Invitation cards for the wedding are printed with this character, many times in gold. It is the character for **JOY** 喜 repeated twice, or 囍 in its original form, which indicates that there is *singing* (⼝

---

* See page W6 (Footnote).　　** See page W6.

mouth) and *music* (a *hand* ⋺ with a *stick* — beating a *drum on a stand* 묘). (**Photos W₃ and W₈**, where it appears on a jar and a flower pot,respectively.)

The good luck sign that can appear on almost any article is 福 for <u>**HAPPINESS**</u>. (**Photos W₁, W₅, W₄** where it appears on an emblem, a kimono, a statue repreting a happy father blessed with a son.) We can explain its meaning by looking at the original form 祒 . The left-hand part represents a *heavenly sign* (＝ *heaven*, and Ⅲ *what comes down from heaven*) *that brings prosperity*; the right-hand part shows *products* ○ *from the field* ⊕ *being under one's roof* ∧ .

As can be expected, the character 愛 for <u>**LOVE**</u> is very popular and very common. (See **Photo W₂** where it appears on a child's dress .) Looking at its ancestral form 愛 we can see the symbol for **Heart** ⱳ that we met before (in **Photo D**): it is a picture of the heart, showing the *sac* (opened), the *lobes* and the *aorta*. Combined with 旡 **To swallow** (a *man* ⋀ *breathing in air* ⹀), it means: **to swallow affectionate feelings down in one's heart.** The other symbol 夊 (*a man* 刀 *who advances in spite of obstacles* ∧) is added to indicate that it is a **lingering feeling.**

Two animals that the Chinese like to use to name their businesses are the <u>**HORSE**</u> 馬 and the <u>**DRAGON**</u> 龍. The original script for the Horse is 馬 , which is a clever picture of the animal, with its mane blowing in the wind. The original form for the Dragon is 龍 . It shows on the left-hand side *the animal* ⺉ *flying towards the sky* ＝ , and on the right-hand side its *wings* ⺃ . The Chinese namely believed that dragons could fly towards the sky and thereby produce rain. As a rule, we find "golden" added as an adjective so that during our walk we'll find "Golden Dragon" as the name for a restaurant (**G**). The character

---

* See page W6 (Footnote).

for **GOLD** is 金, or 金 in its original form. It shows *four gold nuggets* 呈 *buried* (∧ *cover*) *in the ground* * . For Horse, the adjective **PRECIOUS** 寶 is also used. The ancestral form shows *three precious possessions found in one's house* (寶) : *jade* 王 , *porcelain* (缶 *earthenware*) *and money* (貝 *shell*, formerly used as money). **(Photo G – Gold) (Photo T – Precious)**

Let us now take a look at a series of characters that are commonly used by the Chinese, because they deal with the good things in life.

The character for **JOY** is 喜. We met this before in **DOUBLE JOY** **(Photo W3, W6)** Written 喜 it means: *there is music (a hand* 彐 *with a stick* 一 *beating a drum on a stand* 豆 *) and singing (* 口 *mouth*). **(Photo I)** Repeated twice, it is used during wedding celebrations because it is indeed a joyful event for both wife and husband.

Two other common characters 富 **WEALTHY** and 貴 **PRECIOUS, HONORABLE** appear next to each other on a sign for a flower shop. The first was originally written 富 and means: *having products* ○ *of the field* 田 *stacked up* 人 *under one's roof* 宀 . The second was 貴 and means: *a basket* 東 *containing money (* 貝 *shell, formerly used as money), or in other words 'something precious'. **(Photo S)**

---

* If used as a component in a character, it means **Metal** (*four pieces of metal ore buried in the ground*). See, e.g. **Silver**, previously discussed under **BANK**. (See page **W6**)

The next character, 香 means **FRAGRANT** and is closely linked with 港 **HARBOR**, because the two combined mean **HONG KONG**. The original writing for **FRAGRANT** was *繇*, meaning *the sweet* 甘 *(the mouth* 甘 *holding something - agreeable) odor of grain* *來(a plant* 來 *with ripening ears at the top* 丶 *) that is fermenting (* ⌒\ *vapors).* The old writing for **HARBOR** was *圅*, meaning: *water* 水 *and* *何* *what is commonly used (* 廿 *=* ++ *= twenty,* *廾* *pair of hands) in the city* 邑 *(a city* o *and its seal* 邑 *).* **(Photo N)**

And finally, one character with a very positive tone: **PEACE** 平, which was originally written 平, meaning *the breath* 丂 *going through an obstacle — and spreading out freely and evenly* 八. **(Photo M)**

Many times, two or more characters combine to form one meaning(as we have seen earlier with **RESTAU-RANT**, **BANK**, **FIRM**). Here are more examples that we'll meet:

SEAFOOD 海鮮 which is 海 **Sea** (see p. W14) and 鮮 **Fresh** [namely, 魚(**Fish** , picture of a Fish) and 羊 (**Sheep****), which were eaten raw by the ancient Chinese, and therefore had to be fresh].

WORLD 世界, which is **Generation** 世 (*three times ten* +, which was apparently man's life expectancy at that time) and **Boundary** 界 (*land (* ⊕ *field) and separation* 八 *of men* 丁 *).* **(Photos D,R)**

ASIA 亞 洲, which is 亞 (pronounced *Ya*, it is used for its pronunciation only), and **Continent** 洲 (*water* 水 *and tracts of land through which rivers flow* 巛 *).* **(Photo O)**

---

* It is *man* 人 (W6, Footnote) in a bent position 丁.

** Picture of a sheep (seen from behind), with its *horns* 丫, *four feet and tail* ≠.

NEWSPAPER 日報, which is **Sun, Day** ⊙ (picture of the *sun*) and **Announcement, Newspaper** 報 : *a criminal* (￮ * *to offend, commit crime against man* 大 *)* and *a hand* ⋋ *holding a seal* 卩 : *an official announcement (of a judgement).* **(Photo R)**

TRADE CENTER 商 場 In its original form **Trade** 商 looks like a picture of a human face. But actually it consists of three portions: 言 *words* (*the tongue* 舌 *shown outside the mouth, and* = *the sound produced by it* ; *within* (*an object* ⋏ *entering a certain space* ∩); *and* *two suns* ⊙⊙ (*picture of two suns*). The three portions put together mean *when words are spoken inside a room, lasting several days* : **Trade**. The second character actually means **Arena**, or **Open space**. It was formerly written 場 and means: *land* (土 *earth) and* 昜 (*the sun* 曰 *rising* ∧ *above the horizon – and its rays* 勿 *shining over an open space*). **(Photo N)**

ASSOCIATION 會 館 . The first character means **Society**, earlier written as 會 :*meeting* (∧ three lines coming together) *and words (that* ∪ *which comes out from the mouth* ∪ *) are spoken at the fireside* (⊞ *smoke outlet*) . The second character means **Restaurant**, or **Hall**, formerly written 館 : *a large building* 館 (*building* ∩ *with many steps* 阝 *), where food* 食 (*a pot with contents* ⊖ , *a ladle* ∠ , *and the symbol* ∧ *to suggest 'mixing'* (three lines coming together) *is served*. **(Photo P)**

---

* The symbol ￮ represents a *pestle*, capable of producing a grinding, unpleasant action.
** The layer = from which all things ∣ come out.

Four characters are very common, i.e. 北 NORTH, 南 SOUTH, 東 EAST, and 西 WEST. We can easily derive their meanings from their ancestral forms. NORTH 〃 : *two men turning their backs towards the North.* (Facing the South was a Chinese custom during ceremonies.) SOUTH 〴 : *the area 〳 〱 where vegetation (Ψ plant) expands continuously (ꓕ a pestle; the additional stroke – suggests the idea of repetition or continuity).* EAST 東 : *the sun ⊕ is in the East when it is so low that we can see it shining behind the trees 木 (of the Eastern mountains). WEST 〾 : when birds 〿 sit on their nests ⊠ it is evening and the sun is in the West.* (Photo U: South, North)

During our walk we'll pass the sign "Four Seas". So let us now disscuss characters which mean numbers. The Chinese have very simple symbols for the numbers ONE, TWO, and THREE , which are represented by *one stroke* — (一), *two strokes* 二 (二), and *three strokes* 三 (三). The numbers Four, Six and Eight are given symbols which convey the idea that they are 'even' numbers. FOUR ⊕ *means a quantity that can be divided into two equal portions* (now written 四). (Photo E) SIX ⊕ is the same symbol, but *with a dot added to distinguish it from Four.* The modern brush-written form is 六. EIGHT was the simple symbol)((now written 八), meaning *a quantity consisting of two equal halves.* TEN was a *cross* 十 (now written 十), an appropriate symbol, because Ten is a unit. FIVE is also a unit in China (e.g., as used in the abacus), since we have five fingers on each hand. The old symbol was a *diagonal cross* X , now 五. SEVEN is a unit used in fortune-telling and was written 七 :*a cross with a "tail" to distinguish it from the unit Ten.* It is now written 七. (Photo I) And finally, NINE 九, almost the unit Ten, formerly written 〻 : a "wavy" + (Ten).

北
南
東
西

一
二
三
四
六
八
十
五
七
九

To end our discussion, let us now take a look at a few more common characters. **RULER**, or **EMPRESS** 后 * (*see* **Photo F**) formerly written 后 represents a *man bending over* 后 *to give orders* (口 *mouth) to the people.* **FLOWER** 花 (*see* **Photo S**) formerly written 𠈈 means: *that portion of plants* �� *that has greatly changed* 𠈈 (*a man* 𠆢* *and* 𠤎 *a man-upside-down: a man who 'changed' his position*). **HERBS**, or **MEDICINE** 藥 (**Photo U**) , formerly written 藥 consists of two parts. The first part, the one on top, is the symbol for **grass****ᲸᲸ. The second part 樂 looks very complicated, but it is simply a picture of a musical instrument (*a frame with a drum in the middle and bells on the sides*) and represents **Music**, or **Joy**. The two parts put together mean: *herbs (grass) that restore harmony (music, joy) in our body.* **SEA** 海 (*see* (**Photo E**) was formerly written 海 . This symbol consists of three parts. One part is **Water** 水 put on the left-hand side. The second part is **Mother** 母 (*picture of a woman with prominent breasts*). The third part is **Grass** Ჸ, to give the idea of abundance. The three parts put together mean: *the source of all waters.* **PASTRY**, **CAKES** 餅 (*see* **Photo M**), formerly written 餅 has on the left-hand side the symbol for **Food** 食 that we have encountered many times (see pp. **W**4, **W**5, **W**12) . It represents *a pot with contents* ⊖ , *a ladle* ⟨ , *and the symbol* △ *to suggest 'mixing'* (*three lines coming together*). The right-hand part 幷 means **Harmony**: *two men* 𠈌 *marching in step* == . **TO LEARN** 學 (see **Photo Q**), formerly written 學 represents *a child* 子 *in darkness* ⌂ (*a small room)* *and two hands* 𦥑 *of the master pouring down knowledge* 乂 .

**As a rule, symbols dealing with vegetative material have the symbol for *grass* ᲸᲸ added on top.

 * See page W6 (Footnote).

Common Characters in Chinatown (1)

Character & Meaning *	References to Photos **
四 Four[4]	E (Four Seas). 12
七 Seven[7]	I (Chat Hai)
心 Heart[21]	D (World Pastry). L. 2. 23
后 Empress[46]	F (Empress China)
馬 Horse[54]	T (Young's Cafe). 31
龍 Dragon[61]	G (Golden Dragon). 28. 31
花 Flower[68]	S (May's Flowers).
藥 Herbs[72]	U (China Herbs). 7
日 Sun[73]	R (World Journal)
天 Heaven[76]	A (Chinatown Gate)
山 Mountain[86]	4 (Chinese Times). 19
海 Sea[92]	E (Four Seas). T
洲 Continent[94]	O (Asia Garden). 16
金 Gold[96]	G (Golden Dragon)
銀 Silver[97]	C (Bank America)
餐 Meal[104]	H. T (Young's Cafe). 8
飯 Rice[105]	H. L. V. 12 (Szechuan)
粥 Porridge[107]	H. V (Tong Kee)
麵 Noodles[108]	H. V (Tong Kee)
餅 Pastry[112]	M (Ping Yuen)

 * Numbers refer to the Dictionary for its etymology.
 ** The ones with their names are the most illustrative.
 Circle the ones that you know already !

Common Characters in Chinatown (2)

Character & Meaning *	References to Photos **
酒 Wine[115]	B. E. F. G. K. 1. 6, etc.
報 Newspaper[134]	R (World Journal). 4. 19
司 Management[139]	I (Chat Hai). 5. 10. 11
商 Trade[153]	N (Hong Kong). 9. 23
行 Store[157]	C. U. 7. 16. 22 (Banks)
店 Shop[158]	L. S. 12. 13. 17. 32, etc.
家 Household[162]	B. E. G. K. M. 1. 6, etc.
廳 Hall[165]	H. T. 8 (Ping's Place)
園 Garden[166]	B. M (Ping Yuen). O
樓 Story-house[167]	F. 14 (Ming Palace)
宮 Palace[168]	K (Imperial Palace). 14
館 Hall[170]	P (Chinese Association)
會 Society[172]	P (Chinese Association) 9. 15
國 Country[174]	C (Bank America). U. 23
塲 Arena[175]	N (Hong Kong)
港 Harbor[177]	N (Hong Kong)
華 China[180]	B. P. Q. U. 7. 9. 18
中 Center[196]	P. Q. U. 7. 9. 22. 23
下 Below[198]	A (Chinatown Gate)
北 North[200]	U (China Herbs)

* Numbers refer to the Dictionary for its etymology.
** The ones with their names are the most illustrative.
Circle the ones that you know already!

Common Characters in Chinatown (3)

Character & Meaning *	References to Photos **
南 South[201]	U (China Herbs)
大 Big[208]	G (Golden Dragon).10. 21
美 Beautiful[218]	C (Bank America)
香 Fragrant[221]	N (Hong Kong). 6
貴 Honorable[229]	S (May's Flowers)
寶 Precious[230]	T (Young's Cafe). 16
公 Common[234]	A. I (Chat Hai). 5. 10. 11
亞 Ya (Second)[236]	O. 16 (Asia Jewelry)
世 Generation[246]	D. R (World Journal). 2
界 Border[247]	D. R (World Journal). 2
平 Peace[248]	M (Ping Yuen). 17
喜 Joy[256]	I (Chat Hai). 20
富 Wealthy[258]	S (May's Flowers)
福 Happiness[259]	W1. W4. W5 (in windows)
愛 Love[262]	W2 (in windows)
壽 Longevity[264]	W4 (in windows)
囍 Double Joy[268]	W3 (in windows)
財 Wealth[269]	20 (Gung Hay Fat Choy)
學 Learn[272]	Q (Chinese School)
點 Speck[283]	D (World of Patry)

* Numbers refer to the Dictionary for its etymology.
** The ones with their names are the most illustrative.
Circle the ones that you know already !

> *To learn and at due times to repeat what one has learned, is that not, after all, a pleasure ?* **Confucius**

Getting to Know Them – Photo Section

In my other book, *Read Chinese Today*, you became familiar with the 68 most commonly seen characters through questions (and answers) during a walk through San Francisco's Chinatown. This book will help you to increase your knowledge to 288 common characters.

Before we do this, however, we should refresh our knowledge of the 68 characters, by completing the multi-choice questions that go with the Photos A to W. You will find **Walk through San Franciso's Chinatown** on pageW1 in a reduced format; but all key characters are placed in boxes alongside the paragraphs in which they occur. This makes it easy for you to find particular sections frequently referred to.

This section also contains text which introduces **new characters** in the same format that was followed in the "Chinatown Walk"chapter.

In **How to Use the Character Finder and to Find a Character in this Book** (pages P30-31), you will find instructions for writing Chinese characters. This allows you to find the number of strokes in a character, which then allows you to find the meaning and explanation of the character through the **Character Finder** (colored pages).

Practice Page
Write the correct letters on the dotted lines.

			Read from right to left (see W3 and Footnote
A	公 爲* 下 天 A B C		...... Down. Below (W3) ** ...... Common (W3) ...... Heaven (W3)

* 爲 **For (the benefit of)**

		Read
B	華 園 酒 家 A C D	...... Liquor. Wine (W4) ...... Garden (W8) ...... Family. Household (W4) ...... China (W7)

Restaurant: *Wine House*

C	美 國 銀 行 A B C D	...... Country (W8) ...... Beautiful (W8) ...... Store (W6) ...... Silver (W6)

America: *Beautiful Country*   **Bank:** *SilverStore*

** W3 refers to page W3 of the "Chinatown Walk" chapter.

The character for **Heaven** *(in A)* is a very simple one, and so is the one for **Earth** 土 , formerly written 土 : the layer 二 from which all things | come out.

As we have seen, the symbol for **Down** or **Below** *(in A)* is of utmost simplicity. As can be expected, the one for **Up** or **Above** is ⊥ *(an object | above a certain level ―)* , now written as 上 . 上海 W14 is "**Shanghai**" *(above the sea)*.

The character **Common** *(in A)* can be seen many times, because combined with **Management** 司 (W5) it means **FIRM** or **COMPANY**, as we have seen (W5).

Garden *(in B)* stands for **RESTAURANT**, as well as other characters mentioned on W4 and W5. Another one is 廚 , formerly 廚 : *a sheltered place* 广 *: where one pre-* *pares one's meal* 豆 * *(hand* ㄱ *, and* ㄱ *a hand that measures* < ― *measuring stick >)* , normally used by smaller restaurants. Also used for a small restaurant is 室 , formerly 室 , which means **Room**: *a dwelling* 宀 *to which one returns after work* *(a bird* 𡳾 *with wings backward, coming down to earth* 土 [85])*. Also 屋 or 室 means **Room.** The bottom portion is the same as the one just discussed; the top portion means: *a man in a* *sitting, or resting position.*

---

* A simple meal *(• bean)* served on a stemmed platter. Also the symbol for **Bean**[109]

Practice Page
Write the correct letters on the dotted lines.

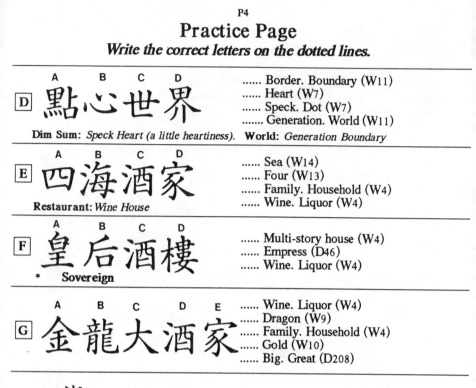

D 點心世界
A B C D

...... Border. Boundary (W11)
...... Heart (W7)
...... Speck. Dot (W7)
.... Generation. World (W11)

Dim Sum: *Speck Heart (a little heartiness).* **World:** *Generation Boundary*

E 四海酒家
A B C D

...... Sea (W14)
...... Four (W13)
...... Family. Household (W4)
...... Wine. Liquor (W4)

Restaurant: *Wine House*

F 皇后酒樓
A B C D

...... Multi-story house (W4)
...... Empress (D46)
...... Wine. Liquor (W4)

* **Sovereign**

G 金龍大酒家
A B C D E

...... Wine. Liquor (W4)
...... Dragon (W9)
...... Family. Household (W4)
...... Gold (W10)
...... Big. Great (D208)

Sea 海 *(Photo E)* can be seen quite often, because combined with **Fresh** 鮮 (W11) they mean **"Seafood"** (W11, *Photo T*). 洋 **Ocean**, formerly 洋 *(water* 氵 *and* 羊 *as "phonetic"),* can be found in 太平洋 **"Pacific Ocean"** *(Very** Peaceful*W11 Ocean).* Many other characters relating to *NATURE* are also commonly used by the Chinese.

洋

Stream or **River** 川 (巛 *a big stream formed by smaller streams)* can be seen combined with **Four** 四 (W13) , because the two mean **"Szechwan"** (the "four rivers province"), a province known also for its cuisine *(Photo12)* Another writing for **River** is 河 (河 *: water* 氵 *and* 可 *as "phonetic").* The **"Yellow River"** is 黃[102] 河.

川

河

Mountain 山 (屾 *picture of a mountain)* is seen many times in San Francisco, because 金山 (Gold W10 Mountain) means **"San Francisco** *(Photos 4 and 19).*

山

Very 太 (大 [208] **Big** with a *dot* added: *"very big".*

Practice Page
Write the correct letters on the dotted lines.

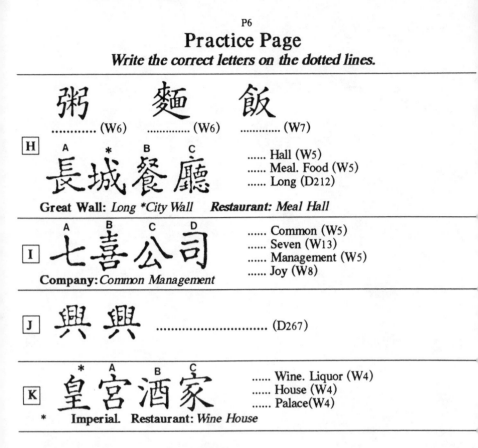

粥 .... (W6) 麵 .... (W6) 飯 .... (W7)

H A 長 * 城 B 餐 C 廳

...... Hall (W5)
...... Meal. Food (W5)
...... Long (D212)

Great Wall: *Long *City Wall*   **Restaurant:** *Meal Hall*

I A 七 B 喜 C 公 D 司

...... Common (W5)
...... Seven (W13)
...... Management (W5)
...... Joy (W8)

Company: *Common Management*

J 興 興 .... (D267)

K * 皇 A 宮 B 酒 C 家

...... Wine. Liquor (W4)
...... House (W4)
...... Palace (W4)

* **Imperial. Restaurant:** *Wine House*

We met **Sun** or **Day** 日 in "Daily Newspaper" *(Photo R)*.
Moon 月 (𝔻 *is a picture of a crescent moon)*. It also means
Month, so that 一 月 means **"January"** (*month one* [W13]).
The symbol for **Star** was 星: *sublimed matter ascending*
∨ *from the earth* 土 [85] *to become stars* ₒ°ₒ : 皇 . *(Photo 5)*.

Water 水 (⺡ *picture of a small stream* \ *with whirls*
of water ⺡ . It can be found in its condensed form 氵 in
characters that represent items of liquid or watery nature. (See,
for example, 酒 Wine[W4], 海 Sea[W14] and 洋 Ocean, 河
River, both discussed on previous page. Also in **Lake** 湖
(*Water* ⺡ *and* 胡 *as "phonetic"),* which can be seen often,
because 湖南 [W13] *(South Lake)* means **"Hunan",** as in
"Hunan Restaurant".

月
星
水
河
湖

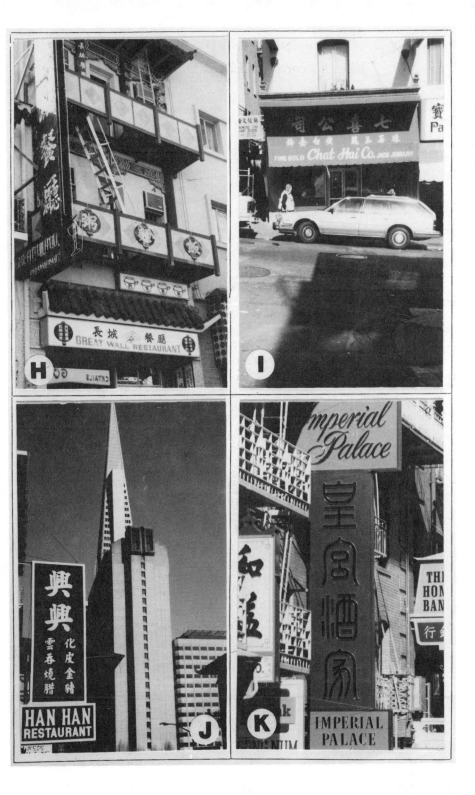

Practice Page
Write the correct letters on the dotted lines.

L	心 樂 飯 店	
	A B C D	...... Shop (W5) ...... Joyful (W14) ...... Heart (W7) ....Cooked rice. Meal (W4)

Restaurant *Meal Shop*

M	平 園 餅 家	
	A B C D	...... Cakes. Pastry (W14) ...... Garden (W4) ...... House (W4) ...... Peace (W11)

N	香 港 商 塲	
	A B C D	...... Harbor (W11) ...... Fragrant (W11) ...... Open space (W12) ...... Trade (W12)

Hong Kong: *Fragrant Harbor*

O	亞 洲 園	
	A B C	...... Garden (W4) ...... *Ya* (W11) * ...... Continent (W11)

* As a rule, this character is only used as a phonetic *(Ya)*. e.g. in 亞洲亞 *(Ya Chou Ya)* to indicate "Asia".

The symbol for **Fire** was *a pile of wood burning with flames:* 火 , now written 火 . **Light** was 光 : *a torch (火 fire) carried by a man* 兀 *(but only his legs are shown)*, now written 光 . **Shadow** 影 was 影 : *shadows* ⁄ *caused by bright light (the sun*[W12] ⊙ *high* 高 *< picture of a tower> up in the sky)*. When combined with 電 (**Electricity,** *see below*), it means "Film", "Motion Picture" 電影 .

Rain was 雨 : *drops of water* == *falling down* | *from clouds* ∩ *suspended from the sky* ⌐ , now written 雨 . **Lightning** or **Electricity** was 電 : *that which extends* ⼹ *from the rain* 雨 *and strikes down* ㇄ , now written 電 . It is a very common character, because with 話 **Talk**, **Speech** (*the tongue* 舌 *and words* == *coming from the tongue* 舌) it means "**Tele-phone**" 電話 *(Photos 24 and 29)*.

Practice Page

Write the correct letters on the dotted lines.

	A	B	C	D	
P	中	華	會	館	...... Society (W12) ...... China (W7) .... Hall (W12) ...... Center (W7)

China: *Center China*   **Association:** *Society Hall*

	A	B	C		
Q	中	華	學	校*	...... Learn (W14) ...... China (W7) ...... Center (W7)

* **School**   **China:** *Center China*

<u>Cloud</u> 雲 was formerly written 雲, meaning: *vapors ⋁ rising to the skies = and producing rain 雨 (see previous page)*. Combined with 吞 **To gulp down** (吞 *to swallow < 口 mouth > in one — big 大 < a person with outstretched arms, as if showing the size of a large object > effort)*, the pair means "**Wonton**", as in "Wonton soup" that popular Chinese dish ("that cloudy delicacy that one gulps down"!).

<u>W</u>ind was 圆 *(insect 虫 < picture of an insect > and air in motion 冫)*. *It was believed that insects were born when the wind blew.* Now written 風 it occurred in combination with 東 **East**[W13] to form "Eastwind" 東 風 , as in "Eastwind Books and Arts" *(Photo 32)*.

Two characters that mean the source of water are: <u> Spring</u> or <u>Fountain</u> 泉 (泉 *water spouting up ⊤ and expanding evenly 水)* and <u>Spring</u> or <u>Source</u> 源 (源 *water 水 and fountain 泉 < see previous character > coming out from the cliff 厂*. The second character has the condensed form of **Water 氵** built in it. *(See also similar characters mentioned at Photos H to K.)*

Finally, under the group **NATURE**, we have <u>Island</u> 島 (島 *a mountain 山 < picture of a mountain > in the sea, on which birds 鳥 can rest while crossing)* . "**Tsingtao beer**" (Green Island beer) is Chinese beer of excellent quality. *(Photo 27)*.

Practice Page
Write the correct letters on the dotted lines.

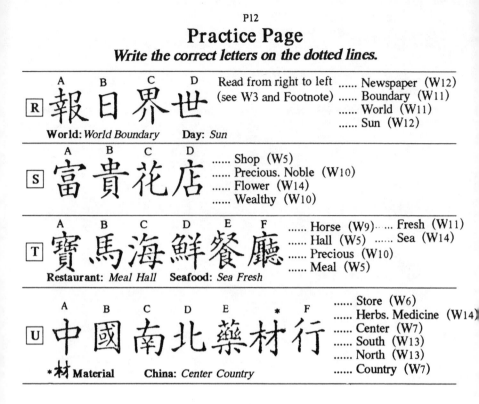

R 報 日 界 世

A   B   C   D

Read from right to left ...... Newspaper (W12)
(see W3 and Footnote) ...... Boundary (W11)
...... World (W11)
...... Sun (W12)

World: *World Boundary*   **Day:** *Sun*

S 富 貴 花 店

A   B   C   D

...... Shop (W5)
...... Precious. Noble (W10)
...... Flower (W14)
...... Wealthy (W10)

T 寶 馬 海 鮮 餐 廳

A   B   C   D   E   F

...... Horse (W9) ... Fresh (W11)
...... Hall (W5) ...... Sea (W14)
...... Precious (W10)
...... Meal (W5)

Restaurant: *Meal Hall*   **Seafood:** *Sea Fresh*

U 中 國 南 北 藥 材 行

A   B   C   D   E   *   F

...... Store (W6)
...... Herbs. Medicine (W14)
...... Center (W7)
...... South (W13)
...... North (W13)
...... Country (W7)

*材 **Material**   **China:** *Center Country*

Other very common characters are 好 **Good, Fine** (好 , which is: *to have a wife 女 and child(ren) 子 (Photo 13)* and **Bright** 明 (明 *the moon* 月 < picture of a crescent moon > shines through the window 日 and the room is brightly lit (Photo 14)*.

Capital 京 was written 京 , which is *a picture of a city-tower.* It can be seen quite often, because 北 W13 京 stands for "Beijing" ("*northern capital*", as opposed to "Nanjing" 南 W13 京 ("*southern capital*").

Two characters are common and often seen. They are 女, which was 女 : *a picture of a woman with a curvy figure* and 男 , which was 男 *the one that gives his strength < 力 picture of a muscle in its sheath > in the field* 田 . They mean **Woman (Female)** and **Man (Male)** and are important, because they indicate restroom facilities, and they may not always be translated for you! *(Photo 33)*.

R 報日界世 WORLD JOURNAL
824 世界書局

S 貴富 店花 812

T 名廚泡製 LUNCH·DINNER FOOD TO GO 397-3455 寶馬海鮮餐廳興 YOUNG'S CAFE

U 中國南北藥材行 CHINA HERBS DAVID'S HAIR DESIGN 時式 CHINA HERBS

Practice Page
Write the correct letters on the dotted lines.

|V| 　　A　　B　　C
粥　麵　飯

...... Rice (plates) (W7)
...... Noodles (W6)
.... Porridge (W6)

|W| 　　A　　B　　C
福　愛　囍

...... Double joy (W8)
...... Happiness. Good fortune (W9)
...... Love (W9)

Here are more characters that are Good Luck Signs.
Wealth 財 (貝∃ *shows a hand* ∃ *that has just brought in money* < 貝 *a shell, formerly used as money* >). You can see this character in 泰喜發財, meaning "Happy New Year!" (*Wishing* [287] *you joy* [256] *and expanding* [288] *wealth* [269]!) (*Photo 20*).

Another one that we see quite often is 安, which means **Peaceful, Secure** (戌 *a woman* 女 *secure within the confines of the house* 宀).

Having our meal in a Chinese restaurant, the waitress will sometimes serve us tea in a teapot with the following inscription 如意吉祥 (*Photo 25*). It means " **According to** one's **Wishes** (意 *expressing one's deep wishes* < 心 *heart* > *through one's words* 言 *, the tongue* 舌 *and* = *the sound produced by it*) :to be **Lucky** (吉 *achieving good fortune, as foretold* < 口 *mouth* > *by a sage* < 士 *one who has knowledge of all things* (*between the two units "one"* — *and "ten"* +)> and **Happy** (祥 *sign coming down* 小 *from heaven* = *proclaiming peace* < 羊 *sheep* [50] >) "

The ancient symbol for **Joy** or **Joyful** is *a picture of a musical instrument* 樂 (*a wooden frame with a drum in the middle and bells on the sides*). Nowadays it is written as 樂 (*Photo L*). When the symbol for **Grass** is put on top, the character means **Medicinal herbs** or **Medicine**, i.e. herbs that restore harmony ("Joy") (*Photo U*).

Practice Page
Write the correct letters on the dotted lines.

	A 壽	B 祥	C 福	
W				...... Happiness. Good fortune (W9) ...... Happiness. Good luck (D257) ...... Longevity (W8)

	福	
W		.... (W9)

	囍	
W		.... (W8)

Here follow other characters that are grouped under the Good Luck Signs in the Dictionary.

誠 (誠 *to accomplish* 成 < *a boy* 亻 *that has reached manhood and can handle the sword* 戈 > *what one has promised* < 言 [273] *words* >): **Sincere. Honest.** *(Photo 3)*.

The symbol for **To prosper** was 興 , which represents *two pair of hands* 𦥑 *lifting up an object in a harmonious way* (同 *agreement: a cover* ⼌ *that perfectly fits a vessel's mouth* 凵). The modern writing is 興 *(Photo 3).*

The character 和 means **Harmonious**, which was written 秝凵, *because it is only natural ("harmonious") for grain* 禾 *(a plant* 朮 *with ripening ears hanging down at the top* 丿 *) to be consumed (* 凵 *mouth) (Photo 11).*

The character for **Good**, **Kind**, **Friendly** is 善 . The ancient writing was 誩, *representing peace (* 羊 [50] *sheep) after a hot dispute (* 言 [273] *words, repeated twice).*

Another one commonly seen is 昌 : **Prosperous, Flourishing**. The ancient form showed *the sun* ⊖ *and the moon* ☽ *(a crescent moon) shining at the same time* 昌 .

As can be expected, some of these characters above are used for names under the assumption that they bring good luck.

Longevity 壽　Prosperity 祿　Happiness 福

Fine PEKING Cloisonné

W₄

W₅

W₆

Practice Page

Write the correct character numbers on the dotted lines.

---

1 金 鳳 酒 家
96 * 115 162

...... Home. House
...... Gold
...... Wine

Restaurant: *Wine House* | *鳳 **Phoenix** |

---

2 世 界 人 參 中 心
246 247 32 * * 195 21

...... Center
...... Boundary
...... World
...... Heart

Center: *Center Heart*

* **Ginseng:** 人參 *(used here as phonetics).* **World:** *World Boundary*

---

3 誠 興
255 267

...... Flourishing
...... Truly. Really

---

4 金 山 時 報
96 86 181 134

...... Newspaper
...... Gold
...... Time
...... Mountain

San Francisco: *Gold Mountain*

---

5 星 河 視 聽 公 司
75 08 * * 234 139

.... Common
... Star
...... Administration   *   **See**   *   **Hear. Rainbow:** *Star River*
...... River   **Company:** *Common Administration*

---

6 一 品 香 酒 家
129 221 115 162

...... House
...... Fragrant
...... One
...... Product

Restaurant: *Wine House*

---

7 萬 華 中 藥 行
13 180 196 72 157

...... Store
...... Ten thousand
...... Center
...... China
...... Herbs. Medicine

All Chinese: *Ten-thousand Chinese*

Practice Page
Write the correct character numbers on the dotted lines.

8 紅 棉 餐 廳
100 71 104 165

...... Hall
...... Red
...... Cotton
...... Meal

Restaurant: *Meal Hall*

---

9 中 華 總 商 會
196 180 * 153 172

...... Association
...... Center
...... China
...... Trade

* **Main. General**   **China:** *Center China*

---

10 大 方 農 產 公 司
208 233 152 151 234 139

...... Administration
...... Big
...... To produce
...... Agriculture
...... Square
...... Common

Company: *Common Administration*

---

11 兆 和 肉 食 公 司
* 249 110 103 234 139

...... Common
...... Harmony
...... Meat
...... Administration
...... Food

* 兆 **Million**   **Company:** *Common Administration*

---

12 四 川 飯 店
4 87 105 158

...... Shop
...... Stream
...... Cooked rice
...... Four

Szechwan: *Four Streams*   **Restaurant:** *Rice Shop*

---

13 好 好 糕 粉 店
215 215 113 111 158

...... Shop
...... Good
...... Flour
...... Pastry

---

14 明 宮 酒 樓
217 188 115 167

...... Liquor. Wine
...... Palace
...... Multi-story house
...... Bright

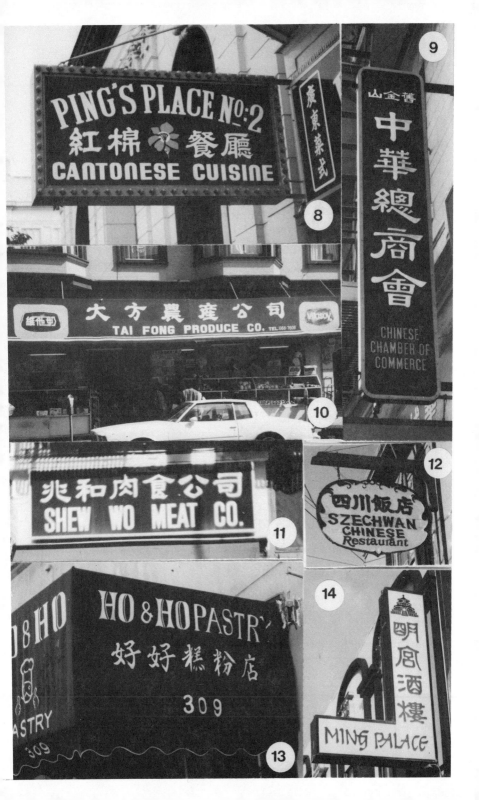

Practice Page
Write the correct character numbers on the dotted lines.

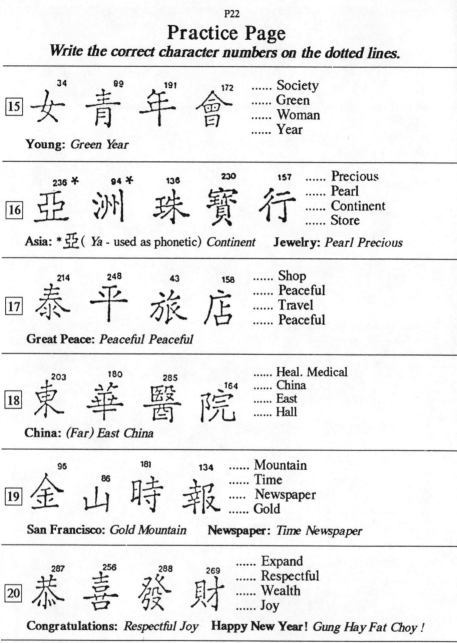

15 女 青 年 會
34 89 191 172

...... Society
...... Green
...... Woman
...... Year

Young: *Green Year*

---

16 亞 洲 珠 寶 行
236 * 94 * 136 230 157

...... Precious
...... Pearl
...... Continent
...... Store

Asia: *亞 (Ya - used as phonetic) Continent*   **Jewelry:** *Pearl Precious*

---

17 泰 平 旅 店
214 248 43 158

...... Shop
...... Peaceful
...... Travel
...... Peaceful

Great Peace: *Peaceful Peaceful*

---

18 東 華 醫 院
203 180 285 164

...... Heal. Medical
...... China
...... East
...... Hall

China: *(Far) East China*

---

19 金 山 時 報
96 86 181 134

...... Mountain
...... Time
...... Newspaper
...... Gold

San Francisco: *Gold Mountain*   **Newspaper:** *Time Newspaper*

---

20 恭 喜 發 財
287 256 288 269

...... Expand
...... Respectful
...... Wealth
...... Joy

Congratulations: *Respectful Joy*   **Happy New Year!** *Gung Hay Fat Choy !*

Practice Page

Write the correct character numbers on the dotted lines.

21 大²⁰⁸ 減* 價¹⁵⁵ ...... Price
...... Big

*減 **Reduce**

22 中¹⁹⁶ 央²⁰⁷ 銀⁹⁷ 行¹⁵⁷ ...... Center
...... Store
...... Silver
...... Center

Central: *Center Center*   **Bank:** *Silver Store*

23 中¹⁹⁶ 國¹⁷⁴ 商¹⁵³ 業¹⁵⁴ 中¹⁹⁶ 心²¹ ...... Trade
...... Heart
...... Country
...... Trade

China: *Center Country*   **Trade:** *Trade Trade*   **Center:** *Center Heart*

24 公²³⁴ 用* 電⁸⁴ 話²⁷⁴ ...... Speech
...... Common. Public
...... Electricity

*用 **Use**   **Telephone:** *Electricity Speech*

25 如* 意²⁵⁰ 吉²⁵³ 祥²⁵⁷ ...... Happiness
...... Fortunate
...... Wish

*如 **As. According to** *("According to your wishes, may you be fortunate and happy !")*

26 米¹⁰⁶ 酒¹¹⁵ ...... Wine
...... Rice

Practice Page

Write the correct character numbers on the dotted lines.

27

青⁹⁹ 島⁹⁵ 哮* 酒¹¹⁵
* 哮 Beer

...... Liquor
...... Island
...... Green

28

九⁹ 龍⁶¹

...... Dragon
...... Nine

29

電⁸⁴ 話²⁷⁴

Telephone: *Electricity Speech*

...... Speech
...... Electricity

30

通²⁴² 血²⁶ 丸¹¹⁸

...... Blood
...... Pill
...... Passage

31
Practice Page
Write the correct character numbers on the dotted lines.

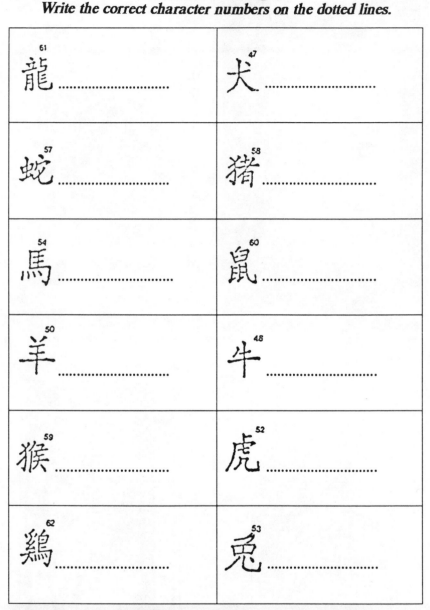

龍 ⁶¹	犬 ⁴⁷ ....
蛇 ⁵⁷	猪 ⁵⁸ ....
馬 ⁵⁴	鼠 ⁶⁰ ....
羊 ⁵⁰	牛 ⁴⁸ ....
猴 ⁵⁹	虎 ⁵² ....
鷄 ⁶²	兎 ⁵³ ....

* *For the correct answers, see "The Chinese Fortune Calendar" on next page. You may also want to write down their ancestral forms .*

THE CHINESE FORTUNE CALENDAR

© K. DARE 1987

810 GRANT AVENUE, SAN FRANCISCO, CA 94108
Tel: (415) 982-8837

How to Use the Character Finder and to Find a Character in this Book.

In the Character Finder (colored pages), the characters in this book are arranged according to the number of their "strokes". A "stroke" is a " straight line" produced by the writing brush without lifting it from the paper.

There are exceptions, however, where a stroke is not a straight line. A stroke can be a "hook", when the brush after writing from left to right, continues writing downward, as in B and C in the example below and as in the first stroke of **Woman** in the example on the next page.

The character 永 for **Perpetually (Always, Forever)**, is a good example of how to write a character and arrive at the number of strokes it consists:

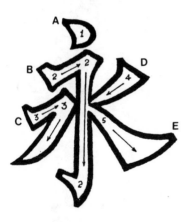

It looks as if this character consists of many strokes, but it actually has only *five* strokes.

This is because B is one stroke only, and so is C. In both cases namely, the writing brush manages to make the "hook" in one continuous movement, without lifting it from the paper.

Can you find the number of strokes of the following characters ?

女	日	金	園	福	愛
Woman	Sun	Gold	Garden	Good luck	Love

You find the answers on the next page !

The number of strokes in a character can best be found by actually writing the character, even if we do so using our finger writing in the air.

There are only a few simple rules to follow. As a rule, strokes are written from from top to bottom or from left to right *. And a character is either built up from left to right or from top to bottom.

The following diagrams should illustrate above rules:

Numbers are the numbers of strokes written so far.
Asterisks (*) are placed near "hooks".

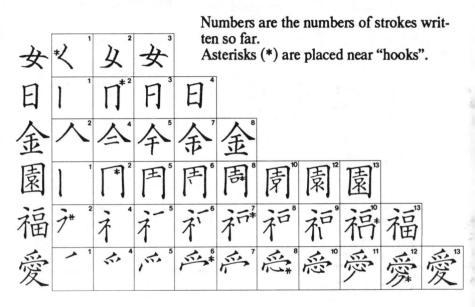

If you can not find the character in the Character Finder, check it in the group with one stroke more or in the group with one stroke less.

In some cases, a character can easily be found without going into the trouble of counting the number of strokes, by looking it up in the appropriate section: **Simple, Intermediate** or **Complex.**

* Unless you are writing with a writing brush, the direction of writing is not of importance. Writing with a brush, it is very important whether you write a stroke from left to right or from right to left, because the resulting "picture" could be very different. For example, to get a stroke that looks the same as D in the example on the previous page, you have to write it from *right to left*.

Let us assume that the photos on the next page are photos that you took yourself during a walk through Chinatown. After you received them from the printer, you want to know the meanings of the characters. Now you have to use the Character Finder. (However, you may know some of the characters already.)

In order to use the Character Finder, you have to know the number of strokes that each character contains. And to know the number of strokes you have to write the characters, as explained to you on the previous two pages. To make it easy for you, here are the characters in the forms you are familiar with.

After having found their meanings, you should enter them on the dotted lines below.

32	東 風 書 店 A B C D	A... B... C... D...
33	女 男 A B	A... B...
34	愛 心 A B	A... B...
35	北 平 園 A B C	A... B... C...
36	塲 車 A B	A... B...
37	字 典 A Records	A...
38	寶 謙 昌 A Modest C	A... C...

WOMEN 女　男 MENS RESTROOM

33

東風書屋
EASTWIND BOOKS & ARTS

32

愛心
HEALTHCARE
PROVIDERS.INC.

34

北
平
園

35

車場

Parking Rates
1/2 Hour $2.
Ea. Add'l hr $2.
Max 24 Hours $13.

PUBLIC

36

The Five Thousand
Dictionary
C. H. Fenn

字典

A Harvard Paperback

37

SUPERIOR
TRADING CO.
寶
謙
昌
參
蔘茸
藥材

38

It would not be a bad idea to circle or highlight in the Character Finder all the characters that you already know. This will make it 'custom-made' for you.

Many times, you can judge the number of strokes of a character by just looking at it, or by using your finger to write in the air. For example, you know by looking at it that No. 40A consists of three strokes, and that No.39C has four strokes. Also, that very complex characters like No. 42A and No.43B belong to the last portion of the Complex Group (Table F).

This means that it is not always necessary for you to count the number of strokes.

39

40

41 金門素食
KOWLOON VEGETARIAN RESTAURANT

42

43

44 CATHAY Kitchen
CHINESE FOOD TO GO
DELIVERY

CHARACTER FINDER

A

Simple

1

一 [1]
One

2

二 [2]
Two

八 [8]
Eight

刀 [116]
Knife

力 [19]
Strength

十 [10]
Ten

九 [9]
Nine

七 [7]
Seven

人 [32]
Man

入 [237]
Enter

3

三 [3]
Three

小 [209]
Small

川 [87]
River

口 [20]
Mouth

山 [86]
Mountain

上 [197]
Above

下 [198]
Below

工 [138]
Work

千 [12]
Thousand

子 [35]
Child

士 [38]
Scholar

土 [85]
Earth

大 [208]
Big.Great

久 [184]
Long.Lasting

夕 [189]
Evening

女 [34]
Woman

丸 [118]
Pill

4

心 [21]
Heart

火 [78]
Fire

水 [77]
Water

化 [279]
Change

六 [6]
Six

元 [148]
Primary.Dollar

父 [36]
Father

分 [186]
Divide.Minute

公 [234]
Public.Common

今 [182]
Now

犬 [47]
Dog

日 [73]
Sun

月 [74]
Moon

王 [44]
King

五 [5]
Five

天 [76]
Heaven

不 [277]
Not.No

方 [233]
Square

文 [270]
Writing.Literature

内 [199]
Inside.Within

少 [15]
Few

止 [240]
Stop

支 [64]
Branch

木 [63]
Tree.Wood

友 [39]
Friend

B

井 117	中 196	午 188	牛 48	手 22	毛 23	5 加 140
Well	Center	Noon	Ox	Hand	Hair	Add

北 200	外 206	永 185	冬 195	司 139	石 123	右 205
North	Outside	Forever.Always	Winter	Manage	Stone	Right

左 204	布 122	包 121	平 248	半 14	母 37	市 178
Left	Cloth	Wrap	Peaceful	Half	Mother	Market

立 241	玉 124	正 226	古 222	去 238	世 246	出 239
Stand	Jade	Correct	Age-old	Go.Leave	World	Go out

本 65	禾 66	田 119	目 27	甘 220	四 4	民 40
Root.Origin	Grain	Field	Eye	Sweet	Four	The people

夹 207	皮 28	矢 120	白 98	生 280		
Center	Skin	Arrow	White	Grow.Live		

Intermediate

竹 [6][67] Bamboo	多 [16] Many	

行 [157] Store	好 [215] Good	合 [149] Agree	全 [216] Complete	吉 [253] Lucky	字 [271] Character	安 [252] Peaceful
至 [183] Until	早 [187] Morning	共 [18] Share	后 [46] Empress	光 [79] Light	虫 [49] Worm.Insect	耳 [25] Ear
百 [11] Hundred	西 [202] West	肉 [110] Meat.Flesh	年 [191] Year	米 [106] Rice	血 [26] Blood	羊 [50] Sheep
舌 [24] Tongue	利 [7][156] Profit	豆 [109] Bean	言 [273] Word	豕 [51] Boar.Pig	每 [17] Every.Each	花 [68] Flower
男 [33] Male. Man	貝 [125] Shell	局 [171] Office	君 [45] Ruler	足 [29] Foot	車 [126] Carriage	
河 [8][88] River	明 [217] Bright	門 [127] Door.Gate	服 [131] Clothes	和 [249] Harmonious	物 [128] Thing.Object	京 [179] Capital
金 [96] Gold	空 [235] Empty.Sky	昌 [254] Prosperous	易 [143] Exchange	青 [99] Green	直 [227] Straight(forward)	店 [158] Shop

D

雨 83 Rain	虎 52 Tiger	夜 190 Night	東 203 East	兔 53 Hare.Rabbit	信 276 Faith	保 150 Protect
洲 94 Continent	洋 93 Ocean	秋 194 Autumn	紅 100 Red	計 141 Calculate	食 103 Food	品 129 Product.Goods
茶 114 Tea	室 160 Room	星 75 Star	春 192 Spring	泉 89 Spring.Fountain	界 247 Boundary	香 221 Fragrant
美 218 Beautiful	風 81 Wind	屋 161 House.Room	南 201 South	面 30 Face	飛 243 Fly	
健 232 Strong.Healthy	海 92 Sea	酒 115 Wine.Liquor	院 164 Courtyard.Hall	祥 257 Good luck	旅 43 Traveler	時 181 Time
珠 136 Pearl	都 173 Metropolis	強 231 Strong	航 244 Navigate	料 142 Raw material	粉 111 Flour	財 269 Wealth
記 275 Remember.Notes	針 133 Needle	高 210 High	華 180 China	宮 168 Palace	家 162 Household	泰 214 Extreme.Peaceful
亞 236 Inferior	夏 193 Summer	恭 287 Respectful	書 132 Book	通 242 Go through	馬 54 Horse	島 95 Island

9

10

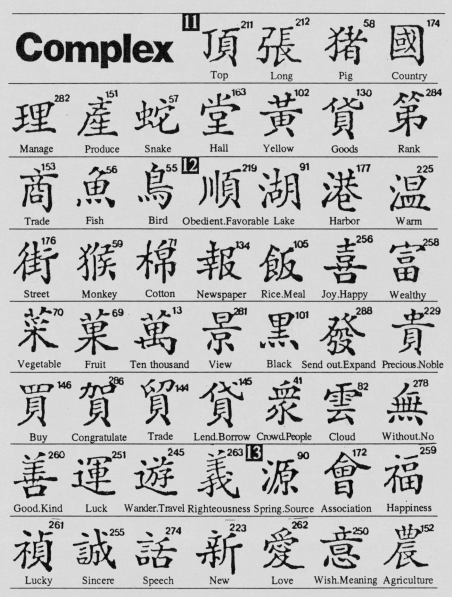

Complex

頂 ²¹¹ Top	張 ²¹² Long		猪 ⁵⁸ Pig		國 ¹⁷⁴ Country	
理 ²⁸² Manage	產 ¹⁵¹ Produce	蛇 ⁵⁷ Snake	堂 ¹⁶³ Hall	黃 ¹⁰² Yellow	貨 ¹³⁰ Goods	第 ²⁸⁴ Rank
商 ¹⁵³ Trade	魚 ⁵⁶ Fish	鳥 ⁵⁵ Bird	順 ²¹⁹ Obedient.Favorable	湖 ⁹¹ Lake	港 ¹⁷⁷ Harbor	溫 ²²⁵ Warm
街 ¹⁷⁶ Street	猴 ⁵⁹ Monkey	棉 ⁷¹ Cotton	報 ¹³⁴ Newspaper	飯 ¹⁰⁵ Rice.Meal	喜 ²⁵⁶ Joy.Happy	富 ²⁵⁸ Wealthy
菜 ⁷⁰ Vegetable	菓 ⁶⁹ Fruit	萬 ¹³ Ten thousand	景 ²⁸¹ View	黑 ¹⁰¹ Black	發 ²⁸⁸ Send out.Expand	貴 ²²⁹ Precious.Noble
買 ¹⁴⁶ Buy	賀 ²⁸⁶ Congratulate	貿 ¹⁴⁴ Trade	貸 ¹⁴⁵ Lend.Borrow	眾 ⁴¹ Crowd.People	雲 ⁸² Cloud	無 ²⁷⁸ Without.No
善 ²⁶⁰ Good.Kind	運 ²⁵¹ Luck	遊 ²⁴⁵ Wander.Travel	義 ²⁶³ Righteousness	源 ⁹⁰ Spring.Source	會 ¹⁷² Association	福 ²⁵⁹ Happiness
禎 ²⁶¹ Lucky	誠 ²⁵⁵ Sincere	話 ²⁷⁴ Speech	新 ²²³ New	愛 ²⁶² Love	意 ²⁵⁰ Wish.Meaning	農 ¹⁵² Agriculture

11 · 12 · 13

E

F

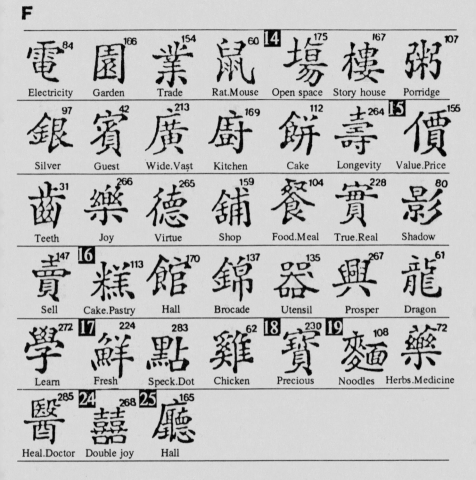

電 84	園 166	業 154	鼠 60	塲 14 175	樓 167	粥 107
Electricity	Garden	Trade	Rat.Mouse	Open space	Story house	Porridge
銀 97	賓 42	廣 213	廚 169	餅 112	壽 264	價 15 155
Silver	Guest	Wide.Vast	Kitchen	Cake	Longevity	Value.Price
齒 31	樂 266	德 265	舖 159	餐 104	實 228	影 80
Teeth	Joy	Virtue	Shop	Food.Meal	True.Real	Shadow
賣 147	糕 16 113	館 170	錦 137	器 135	興 267	龍 61
Sell	Cake.Pastry	Hall	Brocade	Utensil	Prosper	Dragon
學 272	鮮 17 224	點 283	雞 62	寶 18 230	麵 19 108	藥 72
Learn	Fresh	Speck.Dot	Chicken	Precious	Noodles	Herbs.Medicine
醫 285	囍 24 268	廳 25 165				
Heal.Doctor	Double joy	Hall				

Dictionary of
288 Common Characters
explained by their ancestral forms

Ancestral	Explanations	Traditional
	One. One stroke. Photo 6	1
	Two. Two strokes.	2
	Three. Three strokes.	3
	Four. A quantity that can be divided into two equal portions. Photos E. 12	4
	Five. Symbol for a unit. (Five is a unit in China, e.g. as used in the abacus.)	5

1: **One** (*I*). 2: **Two** (*Èrh*). 3: **Three** (San). 4: **Four** (Szù). 5: **Five** (Wû).

Traditional	*Explanations*	*Ancestral*
6	**Six.** A quantity that can be divided into two equal portions. (With a dot added to distinguish it from "Four".)	
7	**Seven.** Symbol for a unit used in divination (with a 'tail' to distinguish it form "Ten"[10]).	
8	**Eight.** A quantity consisting of two equal halves.	
9	**Nine.** Almost a unit: a "wavy" $+$[10]. Photo 28	
10	**Ten.** Symbol for a unit.	

6: **Six** (Liù). 7: **Seven** (*Ch'i*). 8: **Eight** (*Pa*). 9 : **Nine** (*Chîu*). 10: **Ten** (Shíh).

Ancestral	Explanations	Traditional
	Hundred. A unit $-^1$ and White $\ominus^{98}$ as a "phonetic" (Note 1).	11
	Thousand. The symbol for a unit $-^1$ with the symbol for Man ℓ^{32} as a "phonetic" (Note 1).	12
	Ten thousand. Picture of a scorpion, with its head ⊗, legs and tails ⱦ⫠⊓ and its 'thousands' of claws ⱨ. Photo 7 . 43	13
	Half. An Ox $+^{48}$ split ∧ into two equal portions, namely by cutting it lengthwise, the way butchers do.	14
	Few. What is left, after taking away ⱬ a little from somethingthat is already small ノⵏⵌ²⁰⁹.	15

11: **Hundred** (Paî). 12: **Thousand** (Ch'ien). 13: **Ten thousand** (Wàn). 14: **Half** (Pàn). 15. **Few** (Shâo).

<u>NOTE 1</u>: Many symbols consist of two elements: one gives the "idea", the other serves as a "phonetic" (gives the pronunciation).

Traditional	*Explanations*	*Ancestral*
16　多	**Many.** Many nights (two Moons $\mathcal{Z}$[74]).	
17　每	**Each. Every.** Grass ψ , which occurs everywhere, and Mother $\mathcal{R}$[37], to suggest fertility and abundance.	
18　共	**Altogether. To share.** Twenty ⊌(十十[10], connected) hands ⊭⊿ joined together as in a joint effort.	

16: **Many** (*To*). 17: **Each. Every** (*Meî*). 18: **Altogether. To Share** (*Kùng*).

Ancestral	Exlanationns	Traditional
	Sinew. Strength. Picture of a muscle in its sheath. Muscle.	19
	Mouth. Picture of the mouth.	20
	Heart. Picture of the heart: the sac opened; the lobes and the aorta are also seen. Photos D. L. 2. 23 .34	21
	Hand. Picture of the hand with the five fingers clearly shown.	22
	Hair. Picture of a bundle of hair.	23

19: **Sinew. Strength** (*Li*). 20: **Mouth** (*K'ôu*). 21: **Heart** (*Hsin*). 22: **Hand** (*Shôu*). 23: **Hair** (Maó).

Traditional	Explanations	Ancestral
24 舌	**Tongue.** The tongue ♉ shown outside the Mouth ⊔[20].	
25 耳	**Ear.** Picture of the ear.	
26 血	**Blood.** A vase 皿 containing blood – . Photo 30	
27 目	**Eye.** Picture of an Eye*.	
28 皮	**Skin.** The skin ⎰ being stripped off by a hand ⇒ holding a knife ⊃ .	

24: **Tongue** (*Shé*). 25: **Ear** (*Êrh*). 26: **Blood** (*Hsüèh*). 27: **Eye** (*Mù*). 28: **Skin** (*P'í*).

* Originally, it was written horizontally ⊙ ; later it was written vertically to occupy the same space as the other symbols (to maintain uniformity).

Ancestral	*Explanations*	*Traditional*	
	Foot. The foot ⊥, with the ankle, heel and toes. The symbol ○ represents the pelvis.	足	29
	Face. The face with the nose ⊟ in the center.	面	30
	Teeth. Picture of teeth (∞) in an open mouth. (The symbol stop²⁴⁰ ⊔ is added to serve as a "phonetic") (<u>Note 1</u>).	齒	31

29: **Foot** (*Tsú*). 30: **Face** (*Mièn*). 31: **Teeth** (*Ch'ĭh*).

Traditional	Explanations	Ancestral
32 人	**Man.** Originally written with the head and arms shown 头 ; later only the legs are pictured. Photo 2	
33 男	**Man.Male.** The one that gives his strength (力 Sinew[19]) in the Field $\oplus$ [119] . (The female doing her work inside the house.) Photo 33	
34 女	**Woman. Female.** Picture of a woman,with a sexy figure. Photo 33. 15	
35 子	**Child.** Picture of a baby with the legs still bound in swathes.	
36 父	**Father.** A hand ⅎ holding a rod / , to express authority.	

32: **Man** (*Jén*). 33: **Man. Male** (*Nán*). 34: **Woman. Female** (*Nû*). 35: **Child** (*Tzû*). 36: **Father** (*Fù*).

Ancestral	Explanations	Traditional	
	Mother. Picture of a Woman 帑³⁴ with 'breasts' added.	母	37
	Scholar. He who has knowledge of all things (between the two units One —¹ and Ten +¹⁰).	士	38
	Friend. Two hands working in the same direction.	友	39
	People. Weed that grows in abundance (ㄓ and ⁊⁺ are the small stems and leaves). The people.	民	40
	All. The people. A crowd (𠈌³² Men) as observed by the Eye ⊕²⁷· Multitude. The public.	衆	41

37: **Mother** (*Mǔ*). 38: **Scholar** (*Shih*). 39: **Friend** (*Yǔ*). 40: **People** (*Mín*). 41: **All. The people** (*Chùng*).

Traditional	*Explanations*	*Ancestral*
42	**Guest.** Person welcomed into the privacy (由 sitting woman hiding her pregnancy with an apron) of one's house (∧ dwelling) and offered a gift (貝 shell[125], formerly used as money).	
43	**Traveler.** Transients (从[32] Men[32]) seeking shelter under the overhanging branches (∧ of a wind-blown tree ⻖[63]. **To travel.** Photo 17	
44	**King.** The mediator between Heaven ─ , Earth ─, and Man ─.	
45	**Prince.** A hand ⋺ holding a sceptre ╱ and a Mouth 口[20] that makes law. **Monarch.**	
46	**Ruler. Empress.** A Man ∩[32] bending over ╱ to give his orders (口 Mouth[20]) to his people. Photo F	

42: **Guest** (*Pin*). 43: **Traveler** (*Lü*). 44: **King** (*Wáng*). 45: **Prince** (*Chün*). 46: **Ruler. Empress** (*Hoù*)

Ancestral	Explanations	Traditional	
	Dog. Picture of a dog (seen from the front): the two front legs ⟨ and the head with big ear and snout ⊰ turned aside. Photo 31		47
	Ox, Cow. Picture of a cow (seen from behind): only the two hind legs and tail + are seen: the head is shown with the horns Ψ. Photo 31		48
	Worm. Insect. Picture of a worm or insect.		49
	Sheep. Picture of a sheep (seen from behind): the horns Υ, four feet and tail 丰. Photo 31		50
	Pig. Boar. Picture of a pig with a long tail.		51

47: **Dog** (*Ch'ûan*). 48: **Ox. Cow** (*Níu*). 49: **Insect** (*Ch'úng*). 50: **Sheep** (*Yáng*). 51: **Boar** (*Shíh*).

Traditional	Explanations	Ancestral
52 虎	**Tiger.** Representing the stripes ⿱ of the animal and Man 𠘧[32] to indicate it can stand up like a man. Photo 31	
53 兔	**Hare. Rabbit.** Picture of a sitting Hare. Photo 31	
54 馬	**Horse.** Picture of a Horse, with mane blowing in the wind. Photo T. 31	
55 鳥	**Bird.** Picture of a Bird.	
56 魚	**Fish.** Picture of a Fish: head ⼌, scaly body ⊘, and tail ⼆.	

52: **Tiger** (*Hû*).   53: **Hare. Rabbit** (*T'ù*).   54: **Horse** (*Mâ*).   55: **Bird** (*Nĭao*). 56: **Fish** (*Yű*).

Ancestral	*Explanations*	*Traditional*
	Snake. Symbol for a crawling animal (己[49] Worm) and picture of a Snake seen from the front: only its tail and wide-opened mouth with tongue are seen 它 . Photo 31	57
	Pig. Symbol for a Dog 犭 (a sitting dog seen from the side, showing snout, ears and legs) and 者 (a particle) as "phonetic" (see <u>Note 1</u>). Photo 31	58
	Monkey. Symbol for a dog 犭 (see No. 58) and 侯 (Prince) as a "phonetic" (<u>Note 1</u>). Photo 31	59
	Rat. Picture of a Rat (臼 head with whiskers, 鼠 legs and tail). **Mouse.** Photo 31	60
	Dragon. A Dragon 竜 flying towards the sky = and its wings 乚. (It was believed that dragons could fly towards the sky and thereby produced rain.) Photos G. 28. 31	61

57: **Snake** (*Shé*). 58: **Pig** (*Chu*). 59: **Monkey** (*Hóu*). 60: **Rat** (*Shû*). 61: **Dragon** (*Lúng*).

Traditional   **Explanations**   **Ancestral**

雞	**Chicken.** Picture of a bird 🐦 and 🐦 serving as a "phonetic" (<u>Note 1</u>). Photo 31	

62

62: **Chicken** (*Chi*).

Ancestral	Explanations	Traditional
	Tree. Wood. Picture of a tree: the trunk with the branches ∪ and roots ∩ .	木 63
	Branch. Originally written 枝 : it shows a hand ⇒ separating a branch ⼂ from a tree 木[63].	支 64
	Root. Origin. The lower portion of the Tree 木[63], as indicated by the dash − .	本 65
	Grain. A plant (木[63] Tree) with ripening ears hanging down at the top ⼂ .	禾 66
	Bamboo. Picture of a Bamboo tree with drooping leaves.	竹 67

63: **Tree. Wood** (*Mù*). 64:**Branch** (*Chi*). 65: **Root. Origin** (*Pên*). 66: **Grain** (*Hó*). 67: **Bamboo** (*Chú*).

Traditional	Explanations	Ancestral
68 花	**Flower.** The portion of plants ΨΨ that has greatly changed (𝕀𝕌[279] To change). Photo S	
69 菓	**Fruit.** A fruit ⊕ in a tree 朩[63]; and the symbol for grass ΨΨ. (Note 2).	
70 菜	**Vegetables.** A hand that gathers (⌒ profile of a hand reaching down) grass-like (ΨΨ grass) plants (朩[63] Tree). (Note 2). **Dish (food).** Photo 39	
71 棉	**Cotton.** Material from a tree Ψ[63] 朩, from which white θ[98] napkin 巾 is made. Photos 8	
72 藥	**Herbs. Medicine.** Herbs (ΨΨ grass) that restore harmony (⋇[266] musical instrument). Photos U. 7. 42	

68: **Flower** (*Hua*). 69: **Fruit** (*Kuô*). 70: **Vegetables** (*Ts'ai*). 71: **Cotton** (*Míen*). 72: **Herbs. Medicine** (*Yaò*).

NOTE 2: As a rule, symbols dealing with vegetative material have the symbol for "Grass" ΨΨ added on top.

Ancestral	Explanations	Traditional	
⊙	**Sun. Day.** Picture of the Sun. Photo R	日	73
ⅅ	**Moon.** Picture of a crescent Moon.	月	74
(star glyph)	**Star.** Sublimated matter ascending ∪ from the Earth 土[85], to become Stars ₀°₀ . Photo 5	星	75
天	**Heaven.** That which expands ⏤ over Man 大[32]. Photo A	天	76
(water glyph)	**Water. Liquid.** A stream 〈 with whirls of water ⁾⁾ₜₜ .	水	77

73: **Sun** (*Jih*). 74: **Moon** (*Yüèh*). 75: **Star** (*Hsing*). 76: **Heaven** (*T'ien*).
77: **Water** (*Shuî*).

Traditional	Explanations	Ancestral
78 火	**Fire.** A pile of wood burning with flames.	
79 光	**Light.** Fire 火 [78], being carried by a man 儿 [32].	
80 影	**Shadow.** Shadows ⌇ caused by bright light (the sun ☉ [73] high 亢 [210] up in the sky).	
81 風	**Wind.** Motion of air ⌐ and an insect 虫 [49]. (It was believed that all insects were born when the wind blew.)　　　　Photo 32	
82 雲	**Cloud.** Vapors ⌒ rising to the skies ═ and producing rain 雨 [83].	

78: **Fire** (*Huô*). 79: **Light** (*Kuang*). 80: **Shadow** (*Yíng*). 81: **Wind** (*Feng*). 82: **Cloud** (*Yún*).

Ancestral	Explanations	Traditional	
	**Rain.** Drops of water == falling down | from clouds ∩ suspended from the sky 一	雨	83
	**Lightning. Electricity.** That which extends from the rain [83] and strikes down. Photos 24. 29	電	84
	**Earth.** The layer 二 from which all things | come out.	土	85
	**Mountain.** Picture of a mountain. Photos 4. 19	山	86
	**Stream. River.** A big stream formed by smaller streams. Photo 12	川	87

83: **Rain** (*Yû*). 84: **Lightning. Electricity** (*Tièn*). 85: **Earth** (*Tû*). 86:**Mountain** (*Shan*). 87: **Stream. River** (*Ch'uan*).

Traditional	Explanations	Ancestral
88 河	**River.** The symbol for water 巛 and 可 as a "phonetic" (<u>Note 1</u>) Photo 5	河
89 泉	**Fountain. Spring.** Water spouting up ｜ and expanding evenly 几 .	泉
90 源	**Spring.** Water 巛 and fountain 尺 coming out from a cliff ／. **Source.**	源
91 湖	**Lake.** Water 巛 and 胡 as a "phonetic" (<u>Note 1</u>).	湖
92 海	**Sea.** The symbol for water 巛 and 每 every*. Photos E. T . 40	海

88: **River** (*Hó*). 89: **Fountain. Spring** (*Ch'üán*). 90: **Spring** (*Yüán*). 91: **Lake** (*Hú*). 92: **Sea** (*Haî*).

* The bottom part of this symbol is 母 " mother, suggesting that the sea is the "mother" of all waters.

Ancestral	Explanations	Traditional
	Ocean. The symbol for water 水^{77} and 羊^{50} as a "phonetic" (Note 1).	洋 93
	Islets. Continent*. Water 水^{77} and three isles 000 around which water 巛^{87} flows. Photos O. 16	洲 94
	Island. A mountain 山^{86} in the sea, on which birds 鳥^{55} can rest while crossing. Photo 27	島 95
	Gold. Metal. Four nuggets 金 buried ($\wedge$ to cover) in the earth $\pm^{85}$. Photos G. 1. 4. 19. 41	金 96
	Silver. Symbol for metal 金^{96} and 艮 **defiance because silver is malleable (defies the action of a hammer). Photos C. 22	銀 97

93: **Ocean** (*Yáng*). 94: **Islets. Continent** (*Chou*). 95: **Island** (*Taô*). 96: **Gold. Metal** (*Chin*). 97: **Silver** (*Yín*).

* The symbol 000 (many islets combined)could also be interpreted as a large island (continent).

** A man 人^{32} turning around 匕 , in order to look (目^{77} eye) another man "defiantly" in the eye.

Traditional	Explanations	Ancestral
98 白	**White.** The sun $\odot$[73], just rising above the horizon: the sky becoming "white".	
99 青	**Green.** The color (月 a crucible containing a substance colored by heat) of young plants 屮 just growing out from the earth 土[85]. Photos 15. 27	青
100 紅	**Red.** The color of silk 8 (two cocoons on a spindle 丫 being twisted into a silk thread) that requires much work 工[138] to produce. Photo 8	紅
101 黑	**Black.** Soot 义 deposited around the aperture ⊂⊃ by a smoky fire 炎[78].	黑
102 黃	**Yellow.** The fiery glow 炗 (a man 人[32] carrying a torch 火) from the fields 田.	黃

98: **White** (*Pai*). 99: **Green** (*Ch'ing*). 100: **Red** (*Húng*). 101:**Black** (*Hei*). 102: **Yellow** (*Huáng*).

Ancestral	Explanations	Traditional	
	Food. A pot with contents ⊖ , a ladle ⌄ , and the symbol ⌃ to suggest 'mixing' (three lines coming together). Photo 11 . 41		103
	Meal. Food 食[103] and to consume 舛 (彐 a hand and 夂 a skeleton left after the flesh is consumed). **Food.** Photos H. T. 8		104
	Cooked rice. Meal. The symbol for food 食[103] and a hand 彐 in motion ∫ , bringing the food into one's mouth. Photos H. L. V. 12		105
	Rice. Four grains of rice, scattered ✕ due to thrashing + . Photo 26		106
	Porridge. Rice 米[106] that is thoroughly boiled (弱 steam coming from boiling water). Photos H. V		107

103: **Food** (*Shíh*). 104: **Meal** (*Ts'an*). 105: **Cooked rice. Meal** (*Fàn*). 106: **Rice** (*Mî*). 107: **Porridge** (*Chou*).

	Traditional	*Explanations*	*Ancestral*

108	麵	**Noodles.** Wheat 麥 * and 囬 as the "phonetic" (<u>Note 1</u>). Photos H. V	
109	豆	**Bean.** A simple meal • being served on a stemmed platter 豆.	
110	肉	**Meat. Flesh.** Strips of dried meat, bundled together. Photo 11	
111	粉	**Flour.** Rice 米[106] finely ground (川[186] to divide). Photo 13	
112	餅	**Cakes. Pastry.** The symbol for food 食[103] and 并 (two men marching in harmony, suggesting that pastry is a harmonious mixture of ingredients). Photo M	

108: **Noodle** (*Mien*). 109: **Bean** (*Toù*). 110: **Meat. Flesh** (*Jòu*). 111:**Flour** (*Fên*). 112: **Cakes. Pastry** (*Pîng*).

*A plant 朿[83] with ears of grain ⋀ ; and 夊 representing a man 人 who advances in spite of obstacles ⌒ , indicating the relentless development of the grain.

Ancestral	Explanations	Traditional	
糕	**Cakes. Pastry.** Rice 米[106] and 羔 * as the "phonetic" (Note 1). Photo 13	糕	113
茶	**Tea.** Plants ΨΨ and 余 as the "phonetic" (Note 1).	茶	114
酒	**Liquor. Wine.** A liquor jar 酉 and its contents (水[77] water, liquid). Photos B. E .F. G. K. 1. 6. 14. 26. 27	酒	115

113: **Cakes. Pastry** (*Kao*).　114: **Tea** (*Ch'á*).　115: **Liquor. Wine** (*Chîu*).

Traditional	Explanations	Ancestral
116 刀	**Knife.** The ancient form was ⌐刀 ; later the handle was curved upwards for compactness.	𠃌
117 井	**Well. Pit.** A well (the dot •) with eight fields around it to be supplied with water.	⊞井
118 丸	**Pill. Round.** A man ⟨ rolling down a cliff ⟩, suggesting the idea that something has been 'rolled'. **Ball.** Photo 30	刀
119 田	**Field.** Picture of a field with furrows.	⊕
120 矢	**Arrow.** Picture of an arrow.	矢

116: **Knife** (*Tao*). 117: **Well. Pit** (Chîng). 118: **Pill. Round** (Wán). 119: **Field** (*T'íen*). 120: **Arrow** (*Shih*).

Ancestral	Explanations	Traditional	
	Bundle. To wrap. Picture of a foetus 'wrapped' in the womb.	包	121
	Cloth. A napkin ⋔ hanging from the girdle and the symbol ϙ as the "phonetic" (Note 1).	布	122
	Stone. A stone ○ in a cliff ⌐.	石	123
	Jade.* Three pieces of jade ☰ on a string.	玉	124
	Shell. Picture of a small shell ("cowrie").	貝	125

121: **Bundle. To wrap** (*Pao*). 122: **Cloth** (*Pù*). 123: **Stone** (*Shíh*). 124: **Jade** (*Yǜ*). 125: **Shell** (*Pèi*).

Other explanation: 玉 the precious gem • that only Kings 王 could possess.

	Traditional	*Explanations*	*Ancestral*
126		**Carriage.** A carriage (as seen from above), showing the body , axle , and wheels . **Vehicle.** Photo 36	車
127		**Door. Gate.** Picture of a 'saloon-door', with swinging leaves. Photo 41	門
128		**Thing. Commodity.** An ox* [48] and as the "phonetic" (<u>Note 1</u>, p. 3). **Object.**	物
129	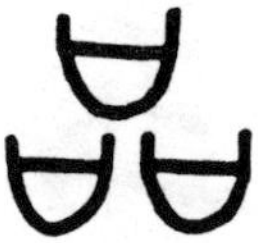	**Product. Goods.** Three objects to represent a multitude of things ([20] mouth, used here only as a symbol for an object). Photo 6	品
130		**Goods.** Things which has to be exchanged ([279] to change) for money ([125] shell, formerly used as money). **Commodities.** Photo 39	貨

126: **Carriage** (*Ch'e*). 127: **Door. Gate** (*Mén*). 128: **Thing. Commodity** (*Wû*). 129: **Product. Goods** (*Pîn*). 130: **Goods** (*Huò*).

* The Ox was a priceless object in China.

Ancestral	*Explanations*	*Traditional*	
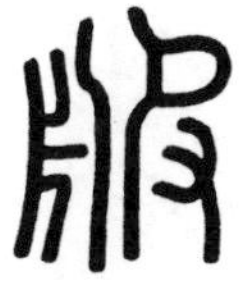	**Clothes. Dress***. A boat governed by a hand holding a scepter .	服	131
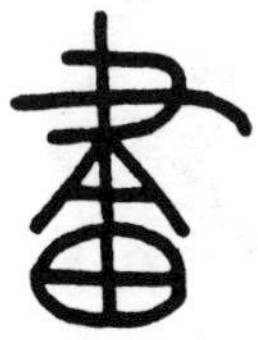	**Book.** A hand holding a stylus drawing a line on a tablet ; and the result of this writing. Photo 32.	書	132
	**Needle.** The symbol for metal [96] and a needle .	針	133
	**Newspaper.** A criminal (** to offend, commit crime against man [32]) and a hand holding a seal : an official announcement (of a judgement). Photos R. 4. 19	報	134
	**Vessel.** Four precious vessels (represented by their mouths [20]) guarded by a dog [47]. **Utensil. Ware.**	器	135

131: **Clothes. Dress** (*Fú*). 132: **Book** (*Shu*). 133: **Needle** (*Chen*). 134: **Newspaper** (*Paò*). 135: **Vessel** (*Ch'ì*).

* The original meaning of this symbol is: "to govern a boat"; there is no satisfactory explanation for the meaning: "dress, clothes".

** The symbol represents a "pestle" (capable of producing a grinding, offensive action).

Traditional	Explanations	Ancestral
136 珠	**Pearl.** A precious stone (王 [124] Jade) and 朱 as the "phonetic" (Note 1). Photo 16	
137 錦	**Brocade.** White 白 [98] cloth 巾 (as in 122) with gold and silver embroidery (金 [96] metal, silver).	

136: **Pearl** (*Chu*). 137: **Brocade** (*Chîn*).

000

000

000

UUUUUUU

Ancestral	Explanations	Traditional	
工	**Work.** The ancient carpenter's square, to symbolize Work.	工	138
司	**To manage. Administration.** A man $\cap^{32}$ bending over $\daleth$ to shout his orders ($\cup^{2c}$ mouth). **Management.** Photos I. 5. 10. 11. 39	司	139
加	**To add.** Strength ($\nearrow^{19}$ sinew) being "added" to the mouth $\cup^{20}$ (namely, while speaking).	加	140
計	**To calculate.** To count ($\equiv^{273}$ to speak) to ten $\dagger^{10}$. **To count.**	計	141
料	**To measure. To calculate.** Measuring rice $\ast^{106}$ with a peck measure ($\dagger^{10}$ ten; $\restriction$ ladle). **Material.**	料	142

138: **Work** (*Kung*). 139: **To manage. Administration** (*Szu*). 140: **To add** (*Chia*). 141: **To calculate** (*Chi*). 142: **To measure. To calculate** (*Liaò*).

Traditional	Explanations	Ancestral
143 易	**To change. To exchange.** Picture of a chameleon - the animal that can change its color.	
144 貿	**Exchange. Trade.** A door 門[127] that is open 𝕎 and money (貝[125] shell, formerly used as money).	
145 貸	**To lend.** Money (貝[125] shell, formerly used as money) being lent and a man 人[32] recording the loan (𝄼 marking pin). **To borrow.**	
146 買	**To buy.** To put something of value (貝[125] shell, formerly used as money) in a shopping net 网.	
147 賣	**To sell.** Putting out 出[239] something of value (貝[125] shell, formerly used as money) that is later placed in a shopping net 网.	

143: **To change. To exchange** (*I*). 144: **Exchange. Trade** (*Maò*). 145: **To lend** (*Tai*). 146: **To buy** (*Maî*). 147: **To sell** (*Mai*).

Ancestral	Explanations	Traditional	
	Beginning. Dollar. The upper portion $=$ of man $\cancel{}$[32]. **Primary.**	元	148
	Agreement. Agreeable. Mouth $\cup$[20] and harmony $\triangle$ (three lines joined together in harmony): words spoken in harmony.	合	149
	To protect. To guarantee. To protect ($\cancel{}$[35] child; and wings of a bird, spread $\wedge\wedge$ to protect its young); and man $\cancel{}$[32](the one to be protected).	保	150
	To produce. To produce ($\cancel{}$[280] to live) and $\wedge$ wrinkles as found on a baby upon birth. Photo 10	產	151
	Agriculture. What is achieved through hard work ($\cancel{}$ two hands; $\cancel{}$ head) at dawn ($\odot$[98] sun and $\cancel{}$ * period). (The symbol for sun $\odot$[98] coincides with $\cancel{}$ head). Photo 10	農	152

148: **Beginning. Dollar** (*Yüán*). 149: **Agreement. Agreeable** (*Hó*). 150: **To protect. To guarantee** (*Pâo*). 151: **To produce** (*Ch'ân*). 152: **Agriculture** (*Núng*).

* A woman who bends over $\cancel{}$ (cp $\cancel{}$[32] man/person in normal position) to conceal her menses (a sitting woman with apron $\cancel{}$).

Traditional	*Explanations*	*Ancestral*
153 商	**Trade.** Where words 言[273] are spoken within 內[199] a room, lasting several days (⊙[98] sun). Photos N. 9. 23	
154 業	**Profession. Trade.** A tree 米[63] crowned with its foliage 业 symbolizing man's activity and its outcome. Photo 23	
155 價	**Value. Price.** The amount determined by the shopkeeper (亻[32] man) to cover (襾 stopper on a bottle) the merhcandise's value (貝[125] shell, formerly used as money). Photo 21	
156 利	**Profit.** When grain 禾[66] is cut (刂[116] knife).	

153: **Trade** (*Shang*). 154: **Profession. Trade** (*Yêh*). 155: **Value. Price** (*Chia*). 156: **Profit** (*Li*). 000: **ppp** (*ppp*).

Ancestral	Explanations	Traditional	
	Store. Footsteps made by left and right feet: a place where people come and go. **Firm.** Photos C. U. 7. 16. 22	行	157
	Shop. A dwelling ⌒ in which divination* is practiced. Photos L. S. 12. 13. 17. 32.	店	158
	Shop. A shed (four walls ▢ under a thatched roof (⌒ roof; ψ plant), and is the "phonetic" (<u>Note 1</u>).	舖	159
	House. Room. A dwelling ⌒ to which one returns after work (⅄ a bird with wings backward, coming down to earth ⊥ 85).	室	160
	House. Room. A place for man to relax (⁊ [32] a man in a sitting position) after work (⅄ a bird coming down to earth ⊥ 85).	屋	161

157: **Store** (*Háng*). 158: **Shop** (*Tièn*). 159: **Shop** (*P'ù*). 160: **House. Room** (*Shih*). 161: **House. Room** (*Wú*).

The symbol ⊦ represents 'cracks' caused by heating tortoise shells. Divination (fortune-telling) was spoken out (▽ [20] mouth) after closely studying the cracks.

Traditional	Explanations	Ancestral
162 家	**Home. Household.** A dwelling ⌂ where pigs 豕 have free entry*. **Family.** Photos B. E. G. K. M. 1. 6	
163 堂	**Hall.** Soil (土 [85] earth) that is being sheltered in a building 坣 (the top portion 𠆢 represents the crest of the roof; ○ is a window).	
164 院	**Hall. Courtyard.** A building with many steps 阝 and 完 as the "phonetic". **Institution.** Photo 18	
165 廳	**Hall. Parlor.** Shelter 广 and as "phonetic" 聽 hear (because musical performance often takes places in a hall). Photos H. T. 8	
166 園	**Garden.** An enclosure ☐ and 袁 a long robe. The latter serves as a "phonetic", but it is also used because the long vines in the garden give the impression that the trees put on robes. Photos B. M. O .35	

162: **Home. Household** (*Chia*). 163: **Hall** (*T'áng*). 164: **Hall. Courtyard** (*Yüàn*). 165: **Hall. Parlor** (*T'ing*). 166: **Garden** (*Yüán*).

* To make sure that they were adequately fed, pigs had the same privileges as dogs today.

Ancestral	*Explanations*	*Traditional*	
	Story-house. Building (tree, wood) and as "phonetic" (a woman locked up in a lofty palace prison for misbehavior). Multi-story building. Photos F. 14	樓	167
	Palace. A dwelling containing a series of rooms . Photos K. 14	宮	168
	Kitchen. A sheltered place , where one prepares one's meal (bean; hand; a hand that measures). Photo 44	廚	169
	Restaurant. Hall. A large building (building with many steps), where food is served. Photo P	館	170
	Office. Bureau. A place where people work: where words (mouth) and hands are used (the span of a hand).	局	171

167: **Story-house** (*Lóu*). 168: **Palace** (*Kuan*). 169: **Kitchen** (*Ch'ú*). 170: **Restaurant. Hall** (*Kuân*). 171: **Office. Bureau** (*Chǘ*).

Traditional	Explanations	Ancestral
172	**Society.** A meeting (three lines coming together) where words (that ∟ which comes out from the mouth ∪²⁰) are spoken at the fireside (a smoke outlet). Association. Photos P. 9. 15	
173	**Capital. Metropolis.** Symbol for city (a city ○ and its seal) and (a particle) as the "phonetic" part.	
174	**Country.** Country ☐ with its capital ○ that is defended by weapons (halberd). Photos U. 23	
175	**Arena.** Ground (⊥⁸⁵ earth) and (the sun ⊝ rising ∧ above the horizon — and its rays ⋔ shining over an open space). Open space. Field. Photo N .36	
176	**Street.** Footsteps and earth ⊥⁸⁵ : that part of the land on which people walk.	

172: **Society** (*Huì*). 173: **Capital. Metropolis** (*Tu*). 174:**Country** (*Kuó*). 175: **Arena** (*Ch'áng*). 176: **Street** (*Chieh*).

Ancestral	Explanations	Traditional	
	Harbor. Water $\stackrel{77}{\text{}}$ and what is commonly used ($\sqcup$ = $+ + +$ ^{10} = twenty; pair of hands) in the city (city o and its seal). Photo N	港	177
	Market. An open space $\sqcap$ with grass ψ where one obtains $\subset$ his necessities.	市	178
	Capital. Picture of a city-tower.	京	179
	Glorious. China. Leaves and flowers that are expanding $\rightleftharpoons$ (breath ς after passing an obstacle $=$, expanding freely) into full bloom. **Glory.** Photos P. Q. 7. 9. 18. 44	華	180

177: **Harbor** (Kâng).   178: **Market** (*Shih*). 179: **Capital** (*Ching*). 180: **China. Glorious** (*Huá*).

Traditional	Explanations	Ancestral
181	**Time.** The sun θ[73] and ⋛ to measure* the growth of plants ψ . Photos 4. 19	
182	**Now.** Union △ and ㄱ , suggesting the idea that all times unite in the "present".	
183	**Until. To arrive.** A bird with wings backward ⋎ , coming down to earth ±[85].	
184	**Long (time). Lasting.** A man ㄅ[32] during his walk hindered by an obstacle ⟍, thus causing him a delay.	
185	**Perpetual.** Representing 'veins of water in the earth', flowing incessantly. **Always.** Photo 39	

181: **Time** (*Shíh*). 182: **Now** (*Chin*). 183: **Until. To arrive** (*Chih*). 184: **Long. Lasting** (*Chîu*). 185: **Perpetual** (*Yûng*).

* Namely, to 'measure the pulse' (the place on the hand ⋛ indicated by the dash —).

Ancestral	Explanations	Traditional	
	Minute. A knife ⟨[116] divides an object into smaller portions: a "minute" is a small portion of an hour. **Divide.**	分	186
	Morning. When the sun ⊖[73] has risen to the height of a man's helmet ⇦.	早	187
	Noon. An ancient sundial to mark the noon.	午	188
	Evening. A wavy half-moon, just appearing above the horizon.	夕	189
	Night. A man 大[32] lying on his side ⟩ in the evening ⟩[189].	夜	190

186: **Minute** (*Fen*). 187: **Morning** (*Tsâo*). 188: **Noon** (*Wû*). 189: **Evening** (*Hsi*). 190: **Night** (*Yêh*).

Traditional	Explanations	Ancestral
191 年	**Year.** A thousand 来[66] grains 个[12] : it took a year to produce the harvest. Photo 15	
192 春	**Spring.** The sun θ[73] and the sprouting of plants 坐 (屮屮 plants).	
193 夏	**Summer.** A man (represented only by his nose 自) with idle hands 𦥑 walking 夊 at leisure.	
194 秋	**Autumn.** When grain 禾[66] ripens and obtains a fiery (火[78] fire) color.	
195 冬	**Winter.** The end 夂 (a loop at the end of a thread) of the year, when ice 仌 appears.	

191: **Year** (*Nien*). 192: **Spring** (*Ch'un*). 193: **Summer** (*Hsia*). 194: **Autumn** (*Ch'iu*). 195: **Winter** (*Tung*).

Ancestral	Explanations	Traditional	
	Center. A target ⊔ pierced in the center by an arrow │ . Photos P. Q. U. 7. 9. 22. 23		196
	Up. Above. An object │ above a certain level — . Photo 40		197
	Down. Below. An object │ below a certain level ⁻ . Photo A		198
	Within. An object entering 人 a certain space ⌒ . Inside.		199
	North. Two men)(³² turning their backs towards the North. (Facing the South was a Chinese custom during ceremonies.) Photo U .35		200

196: **Center** (*Chung*). 197: **Up. Above** (*Shàng*). 198:**Down. Below** (*Hsìa*).
199: **Within** (*Nèi*). 200: **North** (*Peî*).

Traditional	Explanations	Ancestral
201 南	**South.** The area ⟨ ⟩ where vegetation (Ψ plant) expands continuously (⼂ pestle; the additional stroke — suggests the idea of repetition or continuity). Photo U	
202 西	**West.** When birds ⼅ sit on their nests ⊠ it is evening and the sun is in the West.	
203 東	**East.** The sun ⊖[73] is in the East when it is so low that one can see it behind the trees 木[63] (of the eastern mountains). Photos 18. 32.	
204 左	**Left.** The left hand ⼡ : the one that holds the carpenter's square 工 .	
205 右	**Right.** The right hand ⼁ : the one that is used when eating (⼝[20] mouth).	

201: **South** (Nán). 202: **West** (Hsi). 203: **East** (Tung). 204: **Left** (Tsô).
205: **Right** (Yû).

Ancestral	Explanations	Traditional
	Outside. Divination ⊦ * done in the evening ⌒[189], and therefore not according to ("outside") the rules**. **Foreign.**	外 206
	Center. A man 大[32] standing in the middle of space ⊢⊣ . Photo 22	央 207

206: **Outside** (*Wai*) .   207: **Center** (*Yang*).

*This symbol represents 'cracks' caused when tortoise-shells were heated. Fortune-telling took place by closely studying the cracks.

** To interpret dreams, fortune-telling should take place in the morning following the dream, and not later in the evening of that day.

Traditional	Explanations	Ancestral
208 大	**Big. Great.** A man with outstretched arms, as if showing the size of a large object. Photos G. 10. 21	大
209 小	**Small.*** An object split into two.	川
210 高	**High.** Picture of a tower.	高
211 頂	**Top.** The head 頁 (a nose 自 put on two legs ハ representing a man's head) of a nail ↑ .	頂
212 長	**Long.** Hair 𠤎 so long that it is tied with a band – and a brooch) . Photo H	長

208: **Big. Great** (*Tà*). 209: **Small** (*Hsiâo*). 210:**High** (*Kao*). 211: **Top** (*Tĭng*). 212: **Long** (*Chang*).

* Other explanation: 木 a man standing with his feet put together and his arms showing how "small" an object is.

Ancestral	*Explanations*	*Traditional*
	Wide. Shelter ⌐ and yellow 黄[102] : the yellow hall in the imperial palace was a large hall. **Vast.**	廣 213
	Extensive. Liberal. A man 大[32] struggling in the water (廾 hands; 水[77] water), suggesting the idea of "vastness". Photo 17	泰 214
	Good. When one has a wife (女[34] woman) and children 子[35]. **Fine.** Photo 13	好 215
	Perfect. Complete. When a job (工[138] work) is satisfactorily done (◠ harmony, three lines coming together to form a perfect triangle). **Whole.**	全 216
	Bright. When the moon 月[74] shines through the window ⊘ . **Clear.** Photo 14	明 217

213: **Wide** (*Kuâng*).   214: **Extensive. Liberal** (T'ài).   215: **Good** (*Haô*).
216: **Perfect. Complete** (*Ch'üán*).   217. **Bright** (*Míng*).

Traditional	*Explanations*	*Ancestral*
218 美	**Beautiful.** As is a big sheep (大[208] big; 羊[50] sheep) with fully developed horns. Photo C	美
219 順	**Compliant. Favorable.** Following the flow of the river 川[87], and being able to keep one's head 頁 (represented by a nose 自 put on two legs 儿) above water. Obey. Yield to.	順
220 甘	**Sweet.** The mouth 口[20] holding something – agreeable.	甘
221 香	**Fragrant.** The more ancient symbol is 馫 : the sweet 甘[220] odor of fermented (八 vapors) grain 黍[66]. Photos N. 6	香
222 古	**Old.** That which has passed from mouth to mouth 口[20] over many (十[10] ten) generations. Age-old. Ancient.	古

218: **Beautiful** (*Meî*). 219: **Compliant. Favorable** (*Shùn*). 220: **Sweet** (*Kan*).
221: **Fragrant** (*Hsiang*). 222: **Old** (*Kû*).

Ancestral	Explanations	Traditional	
	New. To cut ($\ulcorner$ axe) branches from the hazel tree (木 tree; 辛 offend*). (Only "newly" cut branches of this tree were used to beat criminals.) Photo 39	新	223
	Fresh. Fish 魚^{56} and 羊^{50} sheep, which were eaten raw by the ancient Chinese and therefore had to be fresh. Photo T	鮮	224
	Warm. Water 水^{77} in a dish 皿 with the sun $\odot^{73}$ shining on it.	溫	225
	Correct. To stop 止^{240} "rightly" at the appropriate limit $-$.	正	226
	True. Ten $+^{10}$ eyes $\ominus^{27}$ looking and finding no fault ($\llcorner$ straight angle). **Straight** (forward).	直	227

223: **New** (*Hsin*).   224: **Fresh** (*Hsien*).   225: **Warm** (*Wen*).   226: **Correct** (*Chèng*).   227: **True** (*Chíh*).

* The symbol 辛 represents a 'pestle' capable of producing a grinding, unpleasant action; $=$ one's superior.

	Traditional	Explanations	Ancestral
228	實	**Real.** Real wealth: having a string of shells (毌 string; 貝[125] shells, formerly used as money) under one's roof 宀 .	
229	貴	**Precious. Honorable.** A basket 臾 containing money (貝[125] shell, formerly used as money). **Costly. Noble.** Photo S	
230	寶	**Precious.** Precious possessions in one's house 宀 : 王[124] jade, porcelain (缶 earthenware) and money (貝[125] shell, formerly used as money). Photos T. 16 . 38	
231	強	**Strong.** A beetle 虽 (虫[49] insect) that bounces up in the air (弓 a Chinese reflex bow)when it falls on its back 厶 .	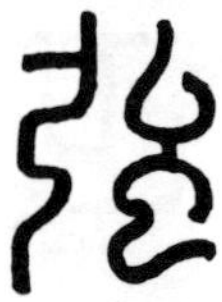
232	健	**Strong. Vigorous.** A man 亻[32] who writes 聿 (a hand 彐 holding a stylus 丨 , writing a line 一 on a table ㅅ) regulations for the march (廴 long strides). **Healthy.**	

228: **Real** (*Shíh*). 229: **Precious. Honorable** (*Kuei*). 230: **Precious** (*Paô*). 231: **Strong** (*Ch'iáng*). 232: **Strong. Vigorous** (*Chièn*).

Ancestral	*Explanations*	*Traditional*
方	**Square.** The ancient form was a swastika 卍 , representing a "square" Earth with the four regions. Photo 10	方 233
公	**Common.** Division and distribution of a private possession (♂ cocoon; with the self-enclosed silkworm it gives the idea of privacy). Public. Photos A. I. 5. 10. 11. 24. 39	公 234
空	**Empty. Hole.** A cavern 穴 dug out by a laborer (工 [08] work).	空 235
亞	**Ugly. Inferior.** The symbol 工[138] (work) badly deformed.* **Second (place).** Photos O. 16	亞 236

233: **Square** (*Fang*). 234: **Common** (*Kung*). 235: **Empty. Hole** (*K'ung*). 236: **Ugly. Inferior** (*Yā*).

* As a rule, this symbol is used as a "phonetic" ("Ya"), as in 亞洲亞[94], which means "Asia".

Traditional	Explanations	Ancestral
237 入	**To enter.** A plant with roots penetrating the soil.	
238 去	**To go.** The lid ⼤ lifted to show an empty vessel ○ : its content "gone". **To leave.**	
239 出	**To go out.** New shoots ⱴ coming out from the mother-plant ⌒.	
240 止	**To stop.** Representing the foot-at-rest, showing toe ⌐ and ankle ⴸ of a foot.	
241 立	**To stand.** A man ⼈[32] standing on the ground — .	

237: **To enter** (*Jù*). 238: **To go** (*Ch'ü*). 239: **To go out** (*Ch'u*). 240: **To stop** (*Chîh*). 241: **To stand** (*Li*).

Ancestral	*Explanations*	*Traditional*	
	Passage. To go through. To march 龰 (止²⁹ foot and 〰 footsteps) and a bud shooting up to a flower 予 . The symbol 用 is used as a "phonetic". Photo 30	通	242
	To fly. Picture of a flying crane.	飛	243
	To navigate. A boat 舟 and the navigator resolutely standing on both legs 介 .	航	244
	To wander. To travel. Proceed 辵 (foot-steps 〰 made by the foot 止²⁹) and 斿 (a man with arms making fluttering motions, swimming aimlessly)*.	遊	245
	Generation. World. Three times ten 十¹⁰: which was apparently man's life's expectancy at that time. Photos D. R. 2	世	246

242: **Passage. To go through** (*T'ung*). 243: **To fly** (*Fei*). 244: **To navigate** (*Háng*). 245: **To wander. To travel** (*Yú*). 246: **Generation. World** (*Shih*).

* The symbol 𦥑 ³⁵ child (with the legs bound in swathes) suggests that the man's legs are not visible, because they are under the water.

Traditional	*Explanations*	*Ancestral*
247 界	**Border. Boundary.** Land ($\oplus$ [119] field) and separation 八 of men ヿ[32].

Photos D. R. 2 | 界 |

247: **Border. Boundary** (*Chièh*).

Ancestral	Explanations	Traditional	
	Even. Peace. The breath ﻉ going through an obstacle — and spreading out evenly 兀. **Peaceful.** Photos M. 17 .35	平	248
	Harmony. It is "harmonious" (natural) that grain 禾⁶⁶ should be consumed (ᵁ²⁰ mouth). **Harmonious.** Photo 11	和	249
	Intention. Wish. Expressing one's intention(ᶜᵧᵧ²¹ heart) by one's words 言²⁷³. **Meaning.** Photo 25	意	250
	To transport. Luck. The Army (an assemblage ∩ of carriages 車¹²⁶) proceeding 辵 (止²⁹ foot; ≋ footsteps) relentlessly.	運	251
	Peaceful. Safe. Women 女³⁴ safe in the house ∩ (dwelling).	安	252

248: **Even. Peace** (*P'íng*). 249: **Harmony** (*Hó*). 250: **Intention. Wish** (*Ì*). 251: **Transport. Luck** (*Yùn*). 252: **Peaceful. Safe** (*An*).

Traditional	Explanations	Ancestral
253 吉	**Fortunate. Lucky.** Achieving good fortune, as foretold (▽²⁰ mouth) by a sage (士³⁸ scholar). Photo 25	吉
254 昌	**Glorious. Prosperous.** Sun ⊖⁷³ and moon ▽⁷⁴ both shining at the same time. Photo 38	
255 誠	**Sincere. Honest.** To accomplish 成 (a boy ↑ that has reached manhood and can handle the sword) what one has promised (²⁷³ words). Photo 3	誠
256 喜	**Joy.** There is singing (▽²⁰ mouth) and music (a hand ⇒ holding a stick — beating a drum on a stand 豆). **Happy.** Photos I. 20	喜
257 祥	**Happiness. Good luck.** Heavenly sign (= heaven; ∭ emanations from heaven) and peacefulness (羊⁵⁰ sheep). Photos W4. 25	祥

253: **Fortunate. Lucky** (*Chí*). 254: **Glorious. Prosperous** (*Ch'ang*). 255: **Truly. Really** (*Ch'éng*). 256: **Joy** (*Hsî*). 257: **Happiness. Good luck** (*Hsíang*).

Ancestral	*Explanations*	*Traditional*	
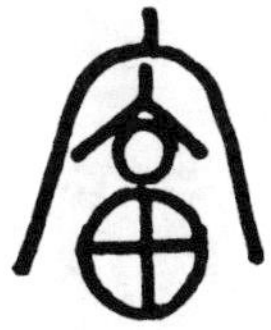	**Wealthy.** Having products ○ of the field ⊕[119] stacked up 人 under one's roof 宀. Photo S	富	258
	**Happiness. Good fortune.** Heavenly sign 示 (= heaven; 川 emanations from heaven) that brings prosperity 畐 (products ○ of the field ⊕[119] being under one's roof 宀). Photos W1. W4. W5	福	259
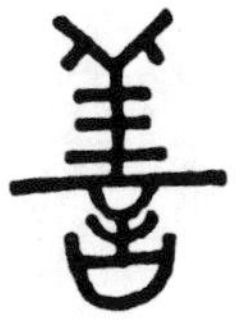	**Good. Kind.** Peace (羊[50] sheep) after a hot dispute (言[273] words). (The more ancient form showed 言[273] repeated twice.) **Benevolent. Charitable**	善	260
	**Lucky. Auspicious.** Heavenly sign 示 (= heaven; 川 emanations from heaven) and money (貝[125] shell, formerly used as money) given to a fortune-teller (卜 cracks in tortoise-shell studied during divination).	禎	261
	**Love.** To swallow 旡* affectionate feelings down in one's heart 心[21]. (The symbol 夊 ** persevere is added to indicate that it is a lingering feeling.) Photo W2.34	愛	262

258: **Wealthy** (*fù*). 259: **Happiness. Good fortune** (*Fú*). 260: **Good. Benevolent** (*Shàn*). 261: **Lucky. Auspicious** (Chen). 262: **Love** (Aì).

* A man 人[32] breathing in air.

** A man 人[32] who advances in spite of an obstacle ∼.

Traditional	Explanations	Ancestral
263 義	**Righteousness.** Peace (¥[50] sheep) following a conflict (two swords crossing each other).	
264 壽	**Longevity.** Old (contraction of [23] hair and [279] change: 'white hair'; furrows, to suggest 'wrinkles') and implore, i.e. to beg (mouth) with gestures (hand) - "longevity" following a deep wish. Photos W4. W6. 43	
265 德	**Virtue.** An upright heart ([27] true and [21] heart) in dealings with, 'going out' (footsteps) to others.	
266 樂	**Music. Joy.** A musical instrument: a frame with a drum (*in the middle*) and bells (*on the sides*). **Joyful. Happy.** Photo L	
267 興	**Prosperous. Flourishing.** Two pairs of hands lifting up an object in a harmonious way (agreement: a cover that perfectly fits a vessel's mouth [20]). Photos J. 3	

263: **Righteousness** [*Yi*). 264: **Longevity** (*Shoù*). 265: **Virtue** (*Té*). 266: **Music. Joy** (Yüèh, Lè). 267: **Prosperous. Flourishing** (Hsing).

Ancestral	Explanations	Traditional	
	Double joy. Joy 喜[256] repeated twice. Photo W3	囍	268
	Wealth. Wealth (貝[125] shell, formerly used as money) acquired (扌 hand). Photo 20	財	269

268: **Double joy** (*xî*). 269: **Wealth** (*zaí*).

Traditional	Explanations	Ancestral
270	**Literature.** Intercrossing lines, representing waves of thought. **Writing.**	
271	**Character.** A child $\stackrel{35}{?}$ carefully reared in the house $\cap$. By extension: a Chinese character, because it generally is the result of careful mixing of smaller units. Photo 37	
272	**Learn. Science.** The child $\stackrel{35}{?}$ in darkness ($\cap$ a small room) and two hands $\stackrel{}{F}\nearrow$ of the master pouring $\stackrel{x}{x}$ knowledge to him. Photo Q	
273	**To speak. Word.** The tongue $\stackrel{24}{\cup}$ and the sound $=$ being produced by it.	
274	**Language. Speech.** Words $\stackrel{273}{\overline{\underline{\Psi}}}$ produced by the tongue $\stackrel{24}{\cup}$. Photos 24. 29	

270: **Literature** (*Wén*). 271: **Character** (*Tzù*). 272: **To learn. Science** (*Hsüéh*). 273: **To speak. Word** (*Yén*). 274: **Language. Speech** (*Huà*).

Ancestral	Explanations	Traditional	
	To remember. Record. Horizontal and vertical threads on a loom 工 (suggesting the idea of "repetition") and 言²⁷³ speak.	記	275
	To believe. Faith. Speak 言²⁷³ and man 人³²: to indicate the words of a man who can be trusted.	信	276
	Not. No. An upward flying bird with wings backward 木 , trying to reach the sky — in vain.	不	277
	Not. Without. A multitude (ㅂㅂ = ++++¹⁰ = forty) of men 大³² clearing a forest (many trees 林林⁶³). Photo 43	無	278
	To change. A man 人³² and a man-upside-down 匕³² : a man who "changed" his position).	化	279

275:To remember. Record (Chì). 276:To believe. Faith (Hsìn). 277:Not.No (Pù). 278:Not. Without (Wú). 279:To change (Huà).

Traditional	Explanations	Ancestral
280 生	**To live.** A plant Ψ growing out from the earth ±[85]. **To grow.**	
281 景	**View.** The sun ☉[73] looking over the capital 京[179].	
282 理	**Principle.** A gem (王[124] jade) which has been cut according to certain "principles", and 里 as "phonetic". **To manage.**	
283 點	**Speck. Dot.** Soot ⊃ᶜ deposited by a smoky (黑[101] black) fire 炎[78] around a vent ⊂⊃ , and 占 as "phonetic". Photo D	
284 第	**Rank.** Thread successively wound 弓 on a spool with a winch at the bottom 升 . **Grade.**	

280: **To live** (*Sheng*). 281: **View** (*Chîng*). 282: **Principle** (*Lî*). 283: **Speck. Dot:** (*Tien*). 284: **Rank** (*Ti*).

Ancestral	Explanations	Traditional	
	Heal. Medical. Drawing out (the hand making a jerky motion) arrows from their receptacle ⌐ , in order to shoot the demon and give elixirs (wine jar) to the patient. Photo 18. **Doctor.**		285
	Congratulate. Wealth ($貝^{125}$ shell, formerly used as money) to be added .		286
	Respect. Respectful. Twenty ⛢ (++^{10} ten) pair of hands joined together and held up as when showing respect ($心^{21}$ heart) to a person as required by Chinese custom. Photo 20		287
	Send forth. Become. To separate (two feet back-to-back) the arrow from the bow . Expand. Photo 20		288

285: **Heal. Medical** (*I*). 286: **Congratulate** (*Hò*). 287: **Respect. Respectful** (*Kung*). 288: **Send forth. Become** (*Fa*).

SUBJECT INDEX

List of Notes

NOTE 1: To avoid having too many symbols, many consist of two symbols: one gives the "idea", the other serves as a "phonetic" (gives the pronunciation). 3

Originally it was written horizontally ⊞ ; later it was written vertically so that it occupies the same writing space as the other symbols. 6

NOTE 2: As a rule, symbols dealing with vegetative material have the symbol for "Grass" ΨΨ added on top. 16

The bottom part of this symbol is 母 mother, suggesting that the sea is the "mother" of all waters. 20

The symbol 𝄞 (many islets combined)could also be interpreted as a large island (continent). 21

A man 人 turning around 𝖢 , in order to look (目 eye) another man "defiantly" in the eye. 21

A plant 屮 with ears of grain ∧∧ ; and 來 representing a man 人 who advances in spite of obstacles ⌢ , indicating the relentless development of the grain. 24

Other explanation: 玉 the precious gem · that only Kings 王 could possess. 27

The Ox was a priceless object in China. 28

The original meaning of this symbol is: "to govern a boat"; there is no satisfactory explanation for the meaning: "dress, clothes". 29

The symbol 午 represents a "pestle" (capable of producing a grinding, offensive action). 29

A woman who bends over 𝖥(cp 人 man/person in normal position) to conceal her menses (a sitting woman with apron 巾). 33

The symbol ⌐ represents 'cracks' caused by heating tortoise shells. Divination (fortune-telling) was spoken out (口 mouth) after closely studying the cracks. 35

To make sure that they were adequately fed, pigs had the same privileges as dogs today. 36

Namely, to 'measure the pulse' (the place on the hand 彐 indicated by the dash —). 40

Other explanation: 八 a man standing with his feet put together and his arms showing how "small" an object is. 46

The symbol 午 represents a 'pestle' capable of producing a grinding, unpleasant action); ═one's superior. 49

As a rule, this symbol is only used as a "phonetic", e.g. in 亞 洲亞 which means "Asia". 51

The symbol 子 child (with the legs bound in swathes) suggests that the man's legs are not visible, because they are under the water. 53

A man 𝖼 breathing in air ≋.57

A man 乃 who advances in spite of an obstacle ⌢ . 57